EXEMPLARY LITERACY TEACHERS

SOLVING PROBLEMS IN THE TEACHING OF LITERACY
Cathy Collins Block, Series Editor

EXEMPLARY LITERACY TEACHERS

Promoting Success
for All Children in Grades K–5

Cathy Collins Block   John N. Mangieri

THE GUILFORD PRESS
New York   London

© 2003 The Guilford Press
A Division of Guilford Publications, Inc.
72 Spring Street, New York, NY 10012
www.guilford.com

Printed in the United States of America

This book is printed on acid-free paper.

Last digit is print number: 9 8 7 6 5 4 3 2 1

Library of Congress Cataloging-in-Publication Data

Block, Cathy Collins.
    Exemplary literacy teachers : promoting success for all children in grades
    K–5 / by Cathy Collins Block & John N. Mangieri.
        p.   cm. — (Solving problems in the teaching of literacy)
    Includes bibliographical references and index.
    ISBN 1-57230-891-5
    1. Language arts (Elementary).   2. Language arts teachers.   I. Mangieri,
John N.   II. Title.   III. Series.
LB1576.B4985 2003
372.6—dc21
                                                                    2003004008

ABOUT THE AUTHORS

Cathy Collins Block, PhD, has served on the Graduate Faculty at Texas Christian University since 1977. She is on the boards of directors of the following organizations: International Reading Association, America Tomorrow, Scientific Literacy Learning (India), and Nobel Learning Communities, Inc. She is on the editorial review boards of *Reading Research Quarterly,* the *Journal of Educational Psychology*, and *The Reading Teacher.* She has directed several nationally funded research projects, and has published more than 95 peer-reviewed research articles on comprehension, classroom instructional interventions, and the professional development of teachers. Her most recent books include *Improving Comprehension Instruction: Rethinking Research, Theory, and Classroom Practice* (coedited, 2003), *Comprehension Instruction: Research-Based Best Practices* (coedited, 2002), *Teaching Comprehension: The Comprehension Process Approach*: (2003), *Literacy Difficulties: Diagnosis and Instruction for Reading Specialists and Classroom Teachers* (2nd edition, 2002), *Scholastic Early Childhood Program* (2002), *Scholastic Kindergarten Reading Program* (2003), and *Scholastic Vocabulary Program Grades 2–6* (coauthored with John N. Mangieri, in press).

John N. Mangieri, PhD, received his doctorate in reading and language arts from the University of Pittsburgh. He has served as the Chairman of the Reading Department at the University of South Carolina, as Dean of the School of Education at Texas Christian University, and has served as the vice-president and president of several universities. Dr. Mangieri, a Fulbright Scholar, is the author or coauthor of 87 professional articles and books. He is the chief author of *Elementary Reading: A Comprehensive Approach* and *Teaching Language Arts Classroom Applications.* He has served as a member of the Classroom Management Committee of the International Reading Association and was the reading representative on the U.S. Office of Education's National Task Force on Urban Education. With Cathy Collins Block, he has been a consultant to "Wishbone," an educational television series for children. Dr. Mangieri presently serves as the Director of the Institute for Literacy Enhancement located in Charlotte, North Carolina.

CONTENTS

EXEMPLARY LITERACY TEACHERS

CHAPTER ONE

DO YOU WANT TO BECOME AN EXEMPLARY LITERACY TEACHER?

Webster's New Collegiate Dictionary defines a teacher as "one whose occupation is to instruct." In that same text, literacy is described as an ability "to read and write."

With these definitions in mind, one would think that it would be an easy task to define an exemplary teacher of literacy. Clearly, such a professional would be an individual who provided instruction in reading and writing in an outstanding manner.

If it is so simple to define an exemplary teacher of literacy, why then are there relatively so few individuals who can be given the label "exemplary"? The answer, of course, lies in the disparity between defining exemplary literacy teaching in abstract terms and the required skills that a professional needs to develop to attain this level of performance.

Why is it important for literacy teachers to be exemplary? Why do so relatively few professionals exhibit the skills required of them to be properly designated as exemplary teachers of literacy? Let us consider each of these questions.

In 1967, data from the National First and Second Grade Studies were reported (Bond and Dykstra, 1997 [1967]). In these investigations, researchers sought to determine which method of reading instruction (e.g., phonics vs. whole-word recognition) was most conducive to student achievement. No single approach was shown to be superior over others in helping children to acquire proficiency in reading.

The other significant finding of this classic, and often cited, study was that the teacher was found to be the key factor in the degree of reading achievement realized by students. Stated another way, children learned to read better with good teaching than with inferior instruction.

After the issuance of this study's findings, a great deal of attention was given to ascertaining the knowledge, skills, and attitudes that teachers needed in order to be able to offer outstanding literacy instruction to students. Perhaps the pinnacle of interest was reached when Dr. Donald L. Cleland, then President of the International Reading

Association (IRA), announced the formation of the Commission on High-Quality Teacher Education in 1970.

This body, cochaired by Dr. Harry W. Sartain and Dr. Paul E. Stanton, was a veritable "who's who" of authorities in the field of reading. The commission reaffirmed that the quality of the teacher was of significant importance to enhanced student achievement in reading. To promote increased quality among teachers, the commission developed a comprehensive list of competencies that teachers needed to possess if high student performance in literacy was to occur.

During the approximately 30 years since this commission issued its report, a great deal of relevant research relating to teachers has been completed. Notable literacy and pedagogy experts such as Robert Ruddell, Gerald Duffy, Barbara Presseisen, David Berliner, and Arthur Costa have developed an important body of information about various facets of teaching that are indicators of quality instruction.

Their work, plus that which preceded it, has consistently reaffirmed the important role that teachers play in student learning. In sum, in the classrooms where exemplary literacy teachers are responsible for instruction, students consistently outperform their counterparts receiving instruction from less skilled teachers.

Our second question—why do comparatively few professionals exhibit the requisite skills to be designated exemplary teachers of reading?—is an intriguing one.

The simple response was once stated on a widely distributed poster. In it, a weary, disheveled person is shown sitting in a chair at the end of a school day. The caption reads: "No one ever said that teaching was going to be easy." As anyone familiar with the profession knows, being a teacher is difficult. Thus, the simple answer is that there are relatively few individuals who can be given the label "exemplary."

Should we be content with the status quo, or should we seek to improve the number of teachers whose teaching can be considered exemplary? We clearly prefer the latter option.

In order for a situation to be improved, it must first be understood. Why is teaching a difficult profession? Teachers are faced with the task of providing *effective instruction to all* students, not merely to children conforming to a particular image. To accomplish this objective, especially at the elementary school level, requires that a teacher meet the individual educational, learning, and human needs of each child.

Accomplishing this feat is not easy. A colleague once remarked, "Schools meet individuals' needs as long as the children are average in intelligence, average in reading ability, and neither introverted or extroverted." Although we have a decidedly more positive viewpoint about schools than our colleague, we do think that she has correctly identified one of the major impediments to excellence in the teaching of literacy to children, namely, the wide range of learners' abilities within a classroom. In a typical elementary school the teacher has the substantial responsibility of providing meaningful instruction not only to students of average ability but also to those with three additional special needs. A brief description of each group follows.

STUDENTS WITH LEARNING DISABILITIES

Court rulings and federal mandates have made it necessary for American elementary schools to educate children who have difficulty in learning. In recent years educators have come to the realization that not all children who fail to learn at a level commensurate with their intellectual potential do so for the same reasons.

Many of these children have been found to possess learning disabilities. The U.S. Congress has defined learning disability as "a disorder in one or more of the basic psychological processes involved in understanding or in using language, spoken or written, . . . may manifest itself in imperfect ability to listen, think, speak, read, write, or spell, or do mathematical calculations" (Public Law 94-142, November 29, 1975). These children are customarily joined in the classroom by students with slow rates of learning.

STUDENTS WITH SLOW LEARNING RATES

In the typical classroom there are children who learn at rates slower than normal. Entire books have been written that discuss the different categories of these students. For our purposes, we will confine our remarks to acknowledging that such children are in our nation's elementary classrooms and that reading is an area in which it is especially difficult for them to gain proficiency. Estimates suggest that some 15% of students cannot quite "keep up" and are usually doing the poorest work in the classroom. It is a teacher's responsibility to provide quality literacy instruction to these students as well as to the ones with markedly different learning needs, specifically, gifted students.

GIFTED STUDENTS

Gifted students are generally of high intelligence and read appreciably above grade level. They do not usually pose severe discipline problems, and they grasp lessons quite quickly. Unfortunately, they often are neglected. Some teachers may be unwittingly "punishing" these children by giving them extra assignments that are of a tedious nature and are not enriching. As a consequence, the students are prevented from enjoyably working up to their capacity.

OTHER FACTORS

Like adults, regardless of whether children have learning disabilities, slow learning rates, or are gifted or average learners, children may be adversely affected by one or more physical maladies or they may be from diverse cultural backgrounds. First we will discuss the physical challenges that confront some children in America's classrooms. We will confine our remarks to the visual and auditory conditions that may affect a child's learning.

Vision

That vision plays a role in a child's learning, especially in reading, is a contention about which none would argue. It is difficult, however, to determine the exact extent to which a particular vision deficit hinders a child's learning. Both vision specialists and educational authorities, however, are in agreement as to the significance of visual discrimination and visual acuity in reading instruction. *Visual discrimination* refers to the ability of a student to discern likenesses and differences among graphic symbols. While visual discrimination is important at all levels of reading, it is particularly significant during the initial stages of literacy instruction. *Visual acuity* is the clarity with which one brings graphic symbols into focus. Students must possess the visual acuity necessary to see adequately both up close and at a distance. When they manifest inadequate visual discrimination and/or acuity and it remains undetected, it makes the task of teaching them even more difficult.

Hearing

Children who have an auditory deficiency usually experience some degree of difficulty in learning, particularly in reading. There are two major ways in which hearing problems inhibit a child from acquiring literacy skills. When a child can hear sounds but cannot differentiate among them, he is said to have an *auditory discrimination* problem. If a child is unable to hear a word or hears the sound in a distorted manner, she has an *auditory acuity* problem.

Regardless of the method used to teach literacy to students, their ability to hear sounds and words correctly and replicate them accurately in subsequent activities is highly important. The child who does not hear sounds correctly will not be able to perform in the same manner as the rest of the class and will probably not profit from phonic instruction. This is particularly true with respect to instruction focusing on consonants. Many consonants require the vocalization of high-frequency sounds, and the majority of hearing problems affect an individual's ability to deal with high-frequency sounds

Cultural Diversity

The very fabric of our nation consists in its being truly a "melting pot," a country in which people from throughout the world immigrate and eventually become citizens. The children of these families come to our nation's classrooms with a multiplicity of linguistic backgrounds. They also vary greatly in their knowledge of the American language. In many parts of the United States, English as a second language (ESL) programs abound for children who often carry a triple burden: (1) for some, their native language has a phonetic base quite different from English; (2) they are faced with learning two languages, one they must speak at home to communicate with family members and the English language that they are learning in schools; and (3) the students do not have a nuclear family support system with language competencies that can help them with homework and reinforce concepts taught at school. Despite the compensating efforts of the professionals who teach these children, many learning gaps go unmet and, as a result, hinder children in their ability to profit fully from instruction.

THE LITERACY CHALLENGE

So far, we have only discussed the teaching profession in general. Now, we would like to offer some insights into specific problems teachers face while trying to provide exemplary literacy instruction.

In conversations we have had with teachers all around the country, one theme has been omnipresent: Teachers are often unfamiliar with specific skills of literacy instruction. Is it any wonder, then, that many of these professionals feel overwhelmed?

In 1974 the IRA's Commission on High-Quality Teacher Education provided an assessment of the knowledge base of beginning elementary teachers, noting:

> Most beginning elementary teachers have been involved in only one or, at best, two brief courses in teaching reading. They know a few of the reading skills that should be taught, and perhaps one method of teaching. But they have little or no knowledge of the limitless number of difficulties that children can encounter in learning to read, of how to diagnose those difficulties, and of the types of instructional adjustments that can be made for different individuals to produce better results. (Sartain & Stanton, 1974, p. 17)

Unfortunately, during the nearly 30 years since this statement was made, little has changed. Some institutions of higher education have improved their teacher education programs in the area of literacy, but the vast majority of them have only made perfunctory changes.

School systems have also done little to help teachers improve their knowledge base about literacy instruction. In many school districts there is no formal reading program. As such, the basal reading series that is being used in the classrooms becomes the de facto reading program. This practice, dubious at best, becomes even more confusing to teachers when, as often happens, a reading series is replaced by one with a vastly different philosophy and reading strategy.

In many school districts, professional development programs in literacy have been poorly funded. When budgets within school districts become constricted, meaningful professional development programs are often the first to be eliminated. Teachers are asked to spend the time normally allocated for this purpose working in their classrooms and/or on planning. Or, they are asked to engage in inane staff-development activities that do not improve their literacy knowledge base.

Even when funds are more plentiful, in most school districts, professional development has often been of a "flavor of the month" variety. Programs are offered based on the whim of a single person, and often this person has limited knowledge about literacy and even less about "best-practices" literacy research. For example, in one school district a staff development program consisted of a person singing western songs—we'll leave it to you to assess how effective that expenditure of funds likely was toward making teachers become more knowledgeable about literacy!

TAKING CHARGE

In the preceding pages we have described past actions that have taken place that have hindered professionals from becoming exemplary teachers of literacy. We have additionally discussed current conditions that adversely affect this objective.

Before we decided to write this book, we were faced with a choice. We could have complained about the challenges that confront literacy instruction and then done nothing more about them. To have reacted that way, however, would be tantamount to surrender. Or, alternatively, we could have taken the attitude that today is be the first day of the rest of one's life in teaching literacy. That is, we could look to find a way out of the current malaise.

We chose the latter course of action. We hope that you will make the same choice: not only to read our words on the remaining pages but also to implement conscientiously the actions that we recommend. Are you ready to take up this challenge and journey with us in an effort to become a better literacy teacher? If so, then please read on . . .

THE WHY?, WHAT?, AND HOW? OF THIS BOOK

You have chosen to begin a process designed to improve your skills as a literacy teacher. We congratulate you for making this decision.

As you read this book, we thought that it would be beneficial if you knew more about the path that will be taken on the subsequent pages. To this end, we would like to share with you the *why* (our rationale for selecting the approach that we use), the *what* (the book's format), and the *how* (the ways the content can be used to help you and your colleagues achieve the goal of becoming a better literacy teacher).

Why?

For the past decade we have been on a mission: we have sought to increase the overall performance of teachers when they provided literacy instruction to students. We also wanted to increase significantly the number of professionals who could legitimately be classified as exemplary teachers of reading.

Despite making some inroads in teacher education as well as professional development programs, our efforts fell well short of reaching the number of educators needed to achieve our goal. We then came to a realization, namely, who could be better qualified to improve the skill levels of teachers than the teachers themselves?

While teachers can't make radical changes in preservice education programs or school district attitudes toward professional development, they *can* change themselves.

After all, teachers are generally bright, dedicated, and sincerely want to do the best job they are capable of.

Once we reached this decision, it quickly became clear what we needed to do. After all, how could professionals become highly effective in literacy instruction if they were unaware of the qualities that exemplary teachers possess?

We decided not to use previously conducted research to determine these qualities. After all, some of these investigations had been conducted many years earlier, while others did not address specifically what we wanted to know; namely, for each grade level from preschool through fifth grade, what qualities distinguished highly effective teachers from less effective peers who taught literacy in the same types of schools?

We sought to learn more about how highly effective teachers create classrooms that maximize students' literacy, and, through use of the research procedure described in Appendix A (which we would urge the reader to review briefly right now), we did just that. Appendix A can also be helpful to individual teachers and educational administrators as they plan professional development sessions. Appendix A summarizes key points in the book grade-level by grade-level, rather than by domains. We have produced data that will answer the question that we just cited. The data show clearly and comprehensively the qualities of outstanding literacy teachers *at each of these grade levels*.

The information we developed provides benchmarks about the qualities of outstanding literacy teachers from preschool though grade 5. Such data can provide preservice teachers with the information essential to make more informed decisions about the specific grade level at which they want to use their talents. As a result, these professionals' skills and abilities can be used more effectively than with the present practice of new teachers designating a more general grade level preference (e.g., primary, intermediate).

This research also can be invaluable to veteran and first-year teachers. These professionals can examine the respective data for the grade that they are presently teaching. If there is a "match" between the qualities of outstanding literacy teachers at this grade level and themselves, then these educators can remain in their present assignments and progress in the profession long enough to accumulate the pedagogical skill and knowledge needed to achieve higher levels of expertise.

If such a match doesn't exist between your present qualities and the grade level at which you are teaching, you have a clear choice. You can elect to remain at that grade level and develop the respective skills and qualities found to be important to literacy teaching effectiveness. Or, you could choose to transfer either up or down to a grade level where your skills are a better fit.

Our profession can be well served by these data in at least three additional ways. First, if teachers engage in the previously described process, fewer of them will become disgruntled and leave education. Second, a better matchup between requirements and abilities will be a major step in providing children with teachers *at each grade level* who can provide outstanding literacy instruction. Finally, in those school districts and states that are employing merit pay systems, a better matchup provides tangible and important criteria upon which classrooms observations can be conducted.

What?

We have opted to write a book that is somewhat different in format and content from others that you may have read. We know that your life—with both school and home responsibilities—is a busy one. Therefore, we made a deliberate attempt to keep the book's length as short as feasible.

We will also write in a nontextbook style. You have chosen to develop professionally in the area of literacy. You and we will be working together in a partnership to attain the objective of your taking an important step to become an outstanding literacy teacher. Our message will be simply but clearly stated in as jargon-free a style of writing as possible.

In subsequent chapters you will be given several opportunities to express your thoughts. For example, in the next chapter we will ask questions about your role as a teacher. In a later chapter you will be asked to complete an assessment. We urge you to give careful thought to these and other activities in this book. Based upon our past experiences with other teachers, we know that these activities can be illuminating. They can also provide you with important data as you seek to enhance your skills as a literacy teacher.

How?

Depending upon your role within schools, the data on subsequent pages may be used in numerous ways.

You can read this book and engage in its content individually, in pairs, or in small groups. After reading the entire text, you should have developed a thorough understanding of your present teaching qualities. You will then also possess knowledge of the attributes of outstanding literacy educators who teach at the same grade level. In instances where disparities exist between your proficiencies and the traits of these teachers, a process for bridging this gap will be presented.

Elementary school principals can use this information to make personnel assignments. Through classroom observations and daily interactions, principals become aware of the qualities that their school's teachers possess and regularly exhibit with children. They are then better prepared to base transfers to other grade levels on knowledge of which teachers have the requisite qualities that are crucial for success in a particular grade.

Principals can also use this information to develop individual growth plans for their personnel. Professionals who may currently lack instructional qualities important to their grade levels can identify the specific areas where they need to show improvement.

Then the principal can support and mentor the teachers as they work to achieve these targeted objectives.

Central administrators can use this book's contents in designing and implementing literacy professional development programs. By designing meaningful opportunities for teacher growth they can initiate a process whereby individuals not only become aware of this data but also use it for improvement. For example, we have written this book in a format that can be easily and effectively employed in schools and districts where book studies regularly occur.

Finally, we have been asked by numerous school districts to conduct professional development sessions for their teachers. This text has served successfully when we lead such programs and when "book studies" have been conducted based on its content.

CONCLUDING THOUGHTS

In 1998 the National Commission on Teaching and America's Future (1998) issued a challenge, after noting that there is a widespread demand "to prepare a new kind of teacher—one who must think harder, longer, deeper—in order to instruct diverse learners in responsive and responsible ways." The challenge consisted in this: "Much is said about what students should know and need to learn in relation to standards, which few literacy educators would dispute (e.g., flexibility in applying different reading strategies), but there is scant information about what teachers actually [do] to develop flexibility among a roomful of diverse learners [from the preschool level through grade 5]."

This book conveys the very content that the National Commission on Teaching and America's Future said was needed. In the next chapter you will take one more step that will get you closer to becoming an exemplary literacy teacher.

CHAPTER TWO

MEMORABLE TEACHERS
Their Legacy

Civilization has long been concerned with the legacy of individuals. For example, Egyptian pharaohs had pyramids constructed so that their entombed remains would be remembered and honored long after their death. In more recent times, colleges and universities have named buildings after their retiring presidents and have permitted wealthy alumni willing to donate large sums of money to have chairs and tenured professorships endowed in their names.

How are teachers remembered? Generally not in structures and buildings, but perhaps in more profound ways.

In Barry Manilow's popular recording "I Write the Songs," he speaks as the personification of music, which, in a sense writes all songs. For teachers, their career's work could be stated as, "I am the professional who teaches all types of students." And, although many might be too humble to say it, some could rightly add: "And I am someone who makes a profound impact on their lives and is remembered fondly by my former students."

If we think back, each of us recalls a teacher (or teachers) about whom the aforementioned could be said. Cathy, one of the coauthors of this book, smiles when she thinks about one of her exemplary literacy teachers, Mrs. McLaughlin. Who is Mrs. McLaughlin? She was Cathy's sixth-grade teacher, a person whom Cathy remembers for her sunny disposition. Mrs. McLaughlin made every child feel special, as though he or she was her very favorite student in the class.

Mrs. McLaughlin was someone whom Cathy and her classmates wanted to please. They knew that books were special to her. She beamed when she taught reading to them. This in part influenced Cathy to adopt a similar attitude toward reading instruction. For her, it became not a chore, but a treat, to read.

When Cathy later became a teacher, Mrs. McLaughlin and two other highly effective teachers continued to be a presence in her life. In planning literacy lessons, Cathy would ask herself: "How would these teachers, especially Mrs. McLaughlin, teach this lesson?" When confronted with students who were reluctant or struggling readers, she would challenge herself to find creative ways to motivate them, just as the exemplary teachers in her life had done.

John, this volume's other coauthor, remembers Sister Gertrude as one of the exemplary teachers in his young life, and as such became his favorite teacher. She was a person who instilled in John and his fellow students a "can-do" attitude about literacy. Sister Gertrude taught higher-level comprehension strategies to all students, whether they had enhanced or limited skills in literacy. She not only exposed them to books of diverse genres but she also expected the students to develop an affinity for these works. Her often repeated line to students was "If you don't believe you can do something, you are the only person in this classroom who feels that way. Because I not only think, but I know, that if you and I both work hard we can accomplish whatever we try to do."

Did Sister Gertrude affect John when he became a teacher? Absolutely. He exhibited that same can-do attitude toward his students that Sister Gertrude demonstrated to him and his classmates.

Success was the prevailing ethos in Sister Gertrude's classroom. Her impact on John extended far beyond the single year that she taught him. As with Mrs. McLaughlin for Cathy, Sister Gertrude and other exemplary literacy teachers served as models upon which John based not only his attitude toward literacy but also his approach to being a teacher.

As you have read the accounts of these teachers who hold a special place in our hearts, you have probably recalled a teacher or two whom you hold in comparable esteem. We would urge you to think about one of those individuals for a few minutes. As you do, ask yourself such questions as: What was it that made this person so memorable? Was it her relationship with you? Or, what actions did he regularly take that made you feel special? Did she help develop in you a special love of reading?

After you have thought about this special teacher in your life, we ask that you stop reading this book and take some time to write about why she or he is so important to you. We ask that you write a few sentences, a paragraph, or whatever you deem appropriate so that you will have a summary of the attributes that made this teacher so significant to you. Space has been provided below for you to accomplish this task. It will take just a moment to write and will prove to be a valuable activity to complete before you turn this page.

THE PRESENT

We have looked into the past to identify teachers who "made a difference" in our lives. Let us now turn our attention to the present—and to you.

Many of us have attended high school reunions. When we haven't seen classmates for several years, we notice changes in them. Some persons look better. Perhaps the once fat kid is now a svelte adult. Or, the person who wore those awful glasses, thanks to either contact lenses or laser surgery, no longer wears them and we notice her beautiful eyes.

At those same reunions, we observe that some individuals' appearance may not have fared very well. For example, their once shapely physiques may have added numerous pounds. Or, someone with a thick head of hair previously may now be bald.

We see the changes in these persons whom we haven't seen for a while. We—who see ourselves daily—often aren't aware of the ways in which we have changed.

What does a high school reunion story have to do with us as teachers? Plenty.

Just as over the years our physical appearance changes, so too does our persona as a teacher. Often the change is evolutionary, taking place in small incremental steps over several years, but in other instances the teacher that we are today may have resulted from a major event that occurred in our lives.

We urge you to think about the teacher that you are at the present time. For example, are you more adept at providing good instruction than you formerly were? Do you still delight in the actions of children, or has your sense of humor drained away over the years? Do you have a positive attitude toward your professional development, or do you regard such efforts as seeking to put "old wine in new bottles"? Do you look forward to each teaching day with a sense of anticipation and joy or, rather, with an attitude of apathy or listlessness?

Answering the question "Who am I as a teacher?" is an important first step toward becoming a more skilled one. We urge you to give careful thought to it. Actions such as introspection and considering the interactions (both positive and negative) that you have had with parents, administrators, and students may provide you with beneficial information in answering this question. Conversations with esteemed colleagues can be an additional source of useful information.

As you engage in this process, remember that a *truthful* and *accurate* answer is your objective. Take precautions to avoid using rationalizations ("If my principal would retire") or alibis ("My students come to school so ill-prepared"). Look at yourself analytically. Remember that you are not trying to impress anyone. Give yourself this baseline information accurately so that it can help you grow as a professional. When you think that you have a clear picture of the teacher that you are *now*, please return to this book and participate in the activities on the following pages.

ACTIVITY ONE: **You through the Eyes of a Student**

Pretend that you are a student in your class. Don't pick one of your favorite students, nor those children with whom you've had conflicts. Rather, choose a student of average ability who fits into neither of the preceding categories. After you have identified the student whom you would be, engage in the following activity.

You have been asked to describe your teacher (in this case, you)—not how the teacher looks but rather how the teacher *acts*. Please write in the space below the things that the teacher does that you like, those things that you dislike, and what you would like to see changed so that he or she would be a better teacher.

ACTIVITY TWO: You, as a Literacy Teacher

We walked into your classroom just as you began to teach literacy that day. We stayed during the entire time that you taught literacy. Write below what we would have heard you say and what we would have seen happen during that period of time.

During that same observation period, write one sentence that describes what you think we would have said is the most important way in which you relate to students.

Describe below what aspect of your teaching style you believe might be detrimental to your effectiveness in providing literacy instruction to students.

ACTIVITY THREE: Literacy Teaching Attribute Analysis

As you consider the content that you have written in Activities One and Two, list below six qualities that you regularly exhibit that most contribute to your students' literacy success.

1.

2.

3.

4.

5.

6.

CONCLUDING COMMENTS

This chapter's exercises have given you a great deal of information about the literacy teacher that you *currently* are. We urge you to reread what you have written on the preceding pages. As you read this material, think about its content so that you have a clear picture of yourself as a teacher.

The process you have just engaged in is an important initial step. In the next chapter you can deepen and broaden your knowledge base. In it, you will be afforded an opportunity to compare your qualities as a literacy instructor to those of exemplary professionals who teach at the same grade level as you.

CHAPTER THREE

NATIONAL EXEMPLARY LITERACY TEACHER ASSESSMENT

In this chapter you will be given an opportunity to learn more about yourself and the manner in which you teach literacy strategies to students. To aid you in acquiring this information, we are going to ask you to complete the National Exemplary Literacy Teacher Assessment (NELTA) later in this chapter. Before you engage in this process, we would like to share a few facts with you.

The NELTA provides data about the significant instructional practices of literacy teachers, and it measures the manner in which you interact with students, select materials, create learning environments, and design lessons. It is divided into two categories. The total score enables you to calculate the degree to which you have already developed the abilities that were exhibited by expert teachers judged to be the most effective in providing instruction for students at your grade level.

In addition, the NELTA provides information that can be helpful as you build new skills in the six domains measured by it. This measure can also assist you in identifying the areas of professional competency that have the greatest potential for your continued literacy instructional growth.

Finally, the NELTA has been administered to numerous literacy teachers who provide instruction at the same grade level as you do. As such, you will be afforded a chance to compare your teaching profile to ones derived from these individuals.

After you complete the NELTA, we will discuss your results as well as how these data can assist you in becoming an even better literacy teacher.

National Exemplary Literacy Teaching Assessment

Instructions: For each item on the National Exemplary Literacy Teaching Assessment, you are to give the response that *most closely* describes the action you would take *first* as a response to the question.

In order to receive optimal benefit from this assessment, you are reminded that it will yield accurate information if, and only if, the responses to the items reflect actual situational frequencies in your literacy teaching. You should not try to guess what response you *should give* to an item. Instead, you are to be as precise as possible in using the alphabetical response that denotes the action that you most frequently employ when teaching reading. Place the letter that denotes your response in the square that precedes each item.

Answer each item as it relates to your most recent literacy teaching experiences. Take as much time as you need to select an accurate response to each item. Remember, there is no right or wrong answer. The value of the information you will receive from the NELTA is directly dependent on the degree to which your responses reflect your teaching actions.

For each item, you are to write the letter that best describes the action that you most often take when the event described in that item occurs in your classroom.

1. When adults enter your classroom during whole-class lessons, they would normally see you:

a. Singing songs, or leading the class in reciting rhyming verses

b. Praising students by complimenting the parts of words that they said correctly while also not emphasizing the parts that were incorrect

c. Teaching literacy all day so that every lesson, regardless of the content area, would include a reading skill that you wanted your students to acquire or utilize

d. Demonstrating the reading process so students could emulate it, regardless of how much prior knowledge they possess

e. Managing a wide variety of groups simultaneously that may be different in size as well as student ability levels

f. Coaching students, whether alone or in small groups, with the goal of motivating and challenging them so that they will attain higher levels of reading achievement

g. Teaching large chunks of knowledge in a manner that motivates students to want to learn

2. If you had to describe the role you most often perform for your students, that role would be as a:

a. Vocational guide—supporting students until they have the ability and confidence to use print on their own

b. Guardian—celebrating students' discoveries and successes as they initially attempt to decode or comprehend

c. Encourager—utilizing many forms of assessments for the purpose of identifying and correcting immediately areas in which students make errors while reading

d. Demonstrator—performing daily at least one "think-aloud," during the introduction of literacy lessons, with a high level of teaching ability

e. Manager—coordinating students as they read multilevel materials whether in small groups, pairs, or alone so that students would be reading at their independent level, or at their instructional level when working with you

f. Coach—introducing a lesson in which students can select from several different options the manner in which they will work to attain the established goal

g. Adaptor—adapting a lesson instantly and successfully because a student indicates that the approach you are using is not working

3. **When you know that the class is becoming unmotivated to read, you would first:**

a. Seek to make that literacy instruction contain more objects found in the child's home

b. Enact the story yourself, or stop and tell a story about the part that is causing difficulty for the class

c. Vary the depth, breadth, and pace of the lesson, teaching up to 20 skills in a single lesson if such an action would keep students engaged

d. Demonstrate how adults would read a particular book and describe what you would enjoy about the book

e. Help students to realize that they can turn to print to locate answers, even though they may lack the confidence that they can do so successfully

f. Create an educational activity that excites students because it relates to an interest/hobby/problem that they have outside of school

g. Bring forward new, intriguing reference material that generates enthusiasm on the part of students that will enable them to become more deeply involved in the subject matter

4. **When you walk into the classroom and see a child who is not motivated to read, you would first:**

a. Go to a shelf and get an object that represents the word or concept you are trying to teach

b. Teach that student the same lesson and read the same book again

c. Have the child read a section to you, praise something read correctly, point out something to improve, ask the child to do it, and indicate that you will be back in a moment to see if it was done correctly by the time you return

d. Initiate on the spot a new creative idea designed to get the unmotivated student to read

e. Hand the student a book written by a new author or of a new genre to try

f. Alter the goal that you had set for the lesson by moving it up or down the cognitive scale based upon the amount that the child understood as you stood by that child's side

g. Ask the students to use what they read to produce something new, which either adds to the classroom, helps their peers, or contributes to the community in which the school is located

5. **You have just completed the best reading lesson that you have ever taught, but as you survey the room, you realize your students have not learned. Their eyes are the blankest you have ever seen! What in the world are you going to do tomorrow to reach them? You plan to:**

a. Create a hands-on activity

b. Repeat the literacy lesson, using the same book in order to attain the same objective

c. Repeat the same lesson, but use a different book, content, or method than you used previously

d. Creatively invent a new way to demonstrate the concept, and explain it in a new way that the students are likely not to have experienced in prior years of schooling

e. Change to a new content area from the one that students were reading so that its new content or genre could stimulate increased interest on their part to build their reading power

f. Teach them how to think on a higher level (e.g., how to draw inferences) as you reteach the concept at a different cognitive level than was utilized previously by you

g. Analyze the critical components of the concept so that you can add another layer of meaning to it that students are not likely to have been taught previously.

6. **If a student asks you a question about a reading skill that you taught yesterday, most often you would:**

a. Use as many learning modalities as feasible in order to answer the question by taking such actions as: letting the student hold an object that represents the concept, writing the words to be learned, asking the student to say the word, saying the word for the child, and finding a way for the student to take physical action consistent with the lesson

b. Call one of the adult volunteers (or teaching assistants) in the room over to talk with the child and to answer all questions about the literacy concept in a one-to-one setting

c. Answer the question immediately, regardless of how insignificant the query

d. Be physically present and educationally supportive until the student finds the answer

e. Stop the class's work briefly, repeat the question so that all can hear it and learn from the masterful answer that you give

f. Praise the student for asking the question, then ask the child whether he or she can identify a resource that can be used to find its answer, and if he or she cannot, prompt the student by taking the first steps in finding the answer to the question

g. Engage the child in a process that you have designed after you have analyzed that student's ability to respond to the question, and after this has occurred, ask the students to explain the process followed to find the answer

7. **Your students respect you. You relate to them exceptionally well. Which of the following actions is most important to you in building and maintaining this rapport?**

a. Creating a class that is as much like a second home for your students as possible

b. Praising correct portions of students' answers rather than telling students what is wrong with their literacy attempts

c. Acknowledging that students are learning while concurrently correcting their slightest errors in a positive manner

d. Listening appreciatively, effectively, and actively when engaged in one-on-one student conferences

e. Taking actions each day that are designed to build an internal value for reading within students

f. Identifying pupils' talents rapidly and focusing your lessons on these talents

g. Using a sense of humor to which students can relate and being able to think like you did when you were their age to understand their motivations

8. **Your students would say that you most value their:**

a. Desire to explore and discover through the use of concrete objects

b. Pace of learning

c. Ability to engage in independent actions

d. Competence in sustaining substantive conversations about literacy

e. Individual reading interests and independent reading ability

f. Willingness to share their ideas about reading, to ask questions, to obtain deeper meanings, and to change their past negative attitudes toward reading to more positive ones

g. Attempts to think "outside the box" as they read, and to express the ideas that were stimulated by this action

9. **When you reflect on the way that you have organized your classroom for literacy instruction, it would best be described in the following way:**

a. Objects you can use to help students relate their oral language to print through the use of smell, taste, touch, and movement are handy

b. Puppets as well as labels for physical objects that can be used to enact stories or to review concepts previously taught

c. Print-rich shelves are at students' level and materials are placed so that students can reach and use them independently

d. Very positive and print-rich—but a relaxed learning environment that challenges students to comprehend on a deeper level than the grade levels that precede the one you teach

e. The wise use of space enables you to work, through your careful management, with a wide range of reading proficiency groups

f. Bulletin boards relating to common, important issues confronting the whole of humanity are prevalent

g. Activities culminate in projects that take longer than a week to complete and these are often designed to be valued/used by others outside the classroom

10. **Which of the following is among the most distinguishing features of your classroom?**

a. Children's hands-on exploration centers (e.g., sufficient space available and objects are used by students to increase their comprehension and appreciation of concepts read)

b. Most of the print and drawings on the bulletin boards will remind us of displays found on the refrigerators of proud parents who frequently display their students' work

c. Trade books and children's literature in every subject are abundant within the classroom as literacy is taught throughout the day

d. Charts demonstrate a wide range of reading abilities, describe how to complete reading processes independently, and teach students to self-correct mistakes when they are reading and writing

e. The class is reading independently, to you, and to each other, and are working in different sizes of groups at one time

f. Visual displays of student products about material read are related to the role that literacy abilities can serve in living a fulfilling life that includes contributing to the welfare of others

g. Your expert planning abilities ensure that all literacy materials are in place before each day's lesson begins and everything runs smoothly even if students' needs dictate changes

11. **If you had to select one of the following, which would be seen most often in the literacy lessons that you teach?**

a. Engaging poems that are printed on charts and that are used for choral reading

b. Pictures that depict a single skill and/or concepts that are being taught during literacy

c. Rapid-paced lessons in which you are sharing in the fun of learning literacy with students

d. Differentiated and highly creative instruction that reflects your need to teach concepts in ways that students would not have been taught in prior years

e. Abstract concepts are made concrete because your directions are clear and effective

f. Many goals and strategies are established at the introduction of lessons so that the students can select their own goals and assume the responsibility for learning them

g. Students have the desire to sign, display, and be identified with their work because you have taught them how to organize their thoughts and to strive for excellence in their literacy tasks

12. **When you ask students to listen to a children's book, you would most likely follow that activity by:**

a. Developing one of the concepts contained in it

b. Matching sounds to print

c. Teaching a word and then, by integrating reading and writing, you would expect students to write this newly taught word

d. Creating word plays and sorting words into categories

e. Mentoring students as they read a related book independently so they will have a high degree of comprehension

f. Focusing subsequent lessons with the goal of students becoming independent readers while working on teacher-generated but student-selected long-term literacy projects related to concepts in the book read

g. Asking students to identify individual interests within the material read and develop a plan for reading more about that topic so as to produce an end product that could be useful to others

CHAPTER FOUR

WHO AM I BEING AS A TEACHER?

In the preceding chapter you were asked to respond to a series of questions contained in the NELTA. Assuming that you responded both candidly and accurately to this assessment's items, you now have important information about your *current* literacy teaching beliefs and behaviors.

So that you can more readily derive information from the NELTA, in this chapter we will ask that you take some additional actions relating to the assessment that you have just completed.

The NELTA contains 12 questions. To continue the assessment, you will record the anwers you gave in Chapter 3 to the NELTA survey here, in Figure 4.1 on the facing page. Figure 4.1 is the Response Summary, which is completed in the following manner. If you gave a response of "d" for question 1 of the NELTA, then place an "×" in the "d" column adjacent to number 1. If for question 2 your answer was a "c," you would put an "×" in the "c" column adjacent to number 2, and so on.

After you have completed Figure 4.1, we then ask that you do the following. Shown below are the grade levels associated with each response (a–g) that you made to the NELTA's items. These are "NELTA Grade Level Teaching Equivalents."

"a"—Preschool
"b"—Kindergarten
"c"—First grade
"d"—Second grade
"e"—Third grade
"f"—Fourth grade
"g"—Fifth grade

Then, in *each* of spaces in Figure 4.2, take these two steps.

1. Next to the NELTA question shown, write the letter (a–g) of your answer to that item in the "Corresponding letter response" column.

FIGURE 4.1. NELTA Response Summary

Question	a	b	c	d	e	f	g
1							
2							
3							
4							
5							
6							
7							
8							
9							
10							
11							
12							

2. In the column adjacent to the aforementioned, place its grade level using the "NELTA Grade Level Teaching Equivalent" previously shown (e.g., a = preschool, b = kindergarten, c = first grade, etc.).

Figure 4.2 provides you with a wealth of important data about the literacy teacher that you are *at present*. To help you better understand the information that they contain, we recommend that you examine these facts about your teaching in two different, but related, ways.

First, we suggest that you look at these data in their totality. A good initial step is to count and record the number of your responses at each grade level to the NELTA questions in Figure 4.3.

Next, we ask that you tally on Figure 4.3 the items that you placed in all of the NELTA Grade Level Teaching Equivalent columns for Figure 4.2. Since there are only

FIGURE 4.2. Domains of the NELTA

Domain 1: Dominant Teaching Roles, Responsibilities, and Talents

NELTA question	Corresponding letter response (a–g)	NELTA Grade Level Teaching Equivalent (preschool–fifth grade)
1.		
2.		

Domain 2: Motivation

NELTA question	Corresponding letter response (a–g)	NELTA Grade Level Teaching Equivalent (preschool–fifth grade)
3.		
4.		

Domain 3: Reteaching

NELTA question	Corresponding letter response (a–g)	NELTA Grade Level Teaching Equivalent (preschool–fifth grade)
5.		
6.		

FIGURE 4.2. *(cont.)*

Domain 4: Relating to students

NELTA question	Corresponding letter response (a–g)	NELTA Grade Level Teaching Equivalent (preschool–fifth grade)
7.		
8.		

Domain 5: Classroom qualities

NELTA question	Corresponding letter response (a–g)	NELTA Grade Level Teaching Equivalent (preschool–fifth grade)
9.		
10.		

Domain 6: Lesson characteristics

NELTA question	Corresponding letter response (a–g)	NELTA Grade Level Teaching Equivalent (preschool–fifth grade)
11.		
12.		

FIGURE 4.3. NELTA Grade Summary

Grade	Number of responses to NELTA questions 1–12
Preschool	
Kindergarten	
First grade	
Second grade	
Third grade	
Fourth grade	
Fifth grade	
Total	

12 items on the NELTA, the *total* number of responses in the "Number of responses to NELTA questions 1–12" column in both Figures 4.3 and 4.4 should be 12.

Figure 4.4 gives you a clear picture as to the efficacy of your present literacy practices relative to the grade level at which you teach. The grade at which you recorded the greatest number of responses indicates the level at which your *present* instructional strategies are most conducive to student literacy growth. The remainder of the information in this column conveys the degree to which other grade-level specific exemplary literacy instructional practices are utilized by you. If there is a tie between the number of responses for any two grade-level teaching equivalencies this tie indicates that you are equally strong in teaching literacies at both of these grade levels. For example, if your highest number of responses was "4" at first and at third-grade level teaching equivalencies, this tie indicates that your talents, philosophies, and values are equally suited to those grades.

What does the "Number of responses" column additionally tell you? If the grade in which you made the highest number of responses is the one at which you are currently teaching literacy, it indicates that you are using strategies that are regularly employed by exemplary literacy teachers at the grade level of your present teaching assignment.

Alternatively, if on Figure 4.4 your highest number of responses were characteristic of a grade other than the one at which you presently teach, these data suggest that your instructional behaviors, teaching skills, and pedagogical actions might be better suited to the literacy needs of students at that grade level, rather than the one to which you are presently assigned.

One other word about these numbers. They also reveal the *degree* to which the skills of a particular grade are imbedded into your *present* literacy practices. NELTA data concerning the highest "Number of responses" (Figure 4.4) show:

- 5–12 responses indicate a "very high" level of strength (the higher the number, the more strength that exists in your instructional practices) in the practices used by exemplary literacy teachers at that designated grade.
- 4 responses indicate a "satisfactory" level of strength
- 3 or fewer responses indicate a "below average" level of strength.

Earlier in this chapter we stated that Figure 4.2 provides you with significant data in two different ways as to the literacy teacher you are at present. The second way in which these figures can help you to better understand the information they convey is by analyzing the domains that they represent.

As you will note, Figure 4.2 divides the NELTA questions into six different do-

FIGURE 4.4. Rank Order of Present Literacy Practices by Grade Level

Responses	Grade (preschool–fifth)	Number of responses to NELTA questions 1–12
Highest number of responses		
Second highest number of responses		
Third highest number of responses		
Fourth highest number of responses		
Fifth highest number of responses		
Sixth highest number of responses		
Fewest number of responses		
Total		

mains. These domains are important in that they constitute the six major competency categories found in our research to be indicative of exemplary literacy teachers in pre-school through fifth grade.

Below you will find explanations of these six important domains.

1. **Dominant Role:** The sets of talents and skills that make up your teaching repertoire; the responsibilities that you assume as a leader in the classroom and the demeanor you exhibit when you teach literacy lessons.
2. **Motivation:** The actions that you take to increase students' desire to read as well as to refocus their interest in becoming better readers.
3. **Reteaching:** The methods you use to plan and implement lessons and assess students when they have not learned a concept the first time that it was taught.
4. **Relating to Students:** The actions that you take to establish rapport with students and to maintain the most positive and amicable learning environment feasible. This domain also includes the strategies that you use to meet individual students' literacy needs.
5. **Classroom Qualities:** The ways in which you organize the desks, furniture, learning materials, books, and teaching aids within your classroom to maximize students' learning.
6. **Lesson Characteristics:** Features, methods, and approaches that are typically employed in the literacy lessons that you teach.

Your responses to the NELTA can give you an accurate profile of your present ways of dealing with each of the six domains. For example, if on questions 1 and 2 your responses were "b" and "d," this indicates that in the domain "Dominant Teaching Roles, Responsibilities, and Talents" you are employing strategies that parallel those of exemplary kindergarten (your "b" response to question 1) and exemplary second-grade (your "d" response to question 2) literacy teachers.

What do these data mean? If, in our example above, you are either a kindergarten or second-grade teacher; the data mean that 50% of your actions regarding "Dominant Teaching Roles, Responsibilities, and Talents" are similar to those strategies regularly used by exemplary teachers at your grade level.

If, in the preceding example, you are a fourth-grade teacher, you did not fare as well. Your responses indicate that in this important domain of literacy instruction, your present teaching actions are more appropriate for these grade levels (kindergarten and second) than for the one that you presently teach (fourth grade).

We ask that you write next to each domain in Figure 4.5 the percentage of your responses that are perfectly congruent with the grade at which you presently teach. To illustrate, in the preceding example you would write 100% next to Domain 1—"Dominant Teaching Roles, Responsibilities, and Talents"—if *both* of your responses on the NELTA were "b" and you teach kindergarten, or for another example, were "c" if you are a first-grade teacher. Similarly, you would write 50% if *one* of your responses to

FIGURE 4.5. Correlation between My Present
Teaching Responsibility and the Actions That I Take

Domain	Percentage of responses that are conducive to "best practices" at the grade I teach
1. Dominant Role	
2. Motivation	
3. Reteaching	
4. Relating to Students	
5. Classroom Qualities	
6. Lesson Characteristics	

questions 1 and 2 matches perfectly the actions of exemplary professionals at the same grade as you teach and 0% if *neither* of your answers agrees with the NELTA formulation. Please fill out the form in Figure 4.5 similarly for all domains at this juncture.

Using the data on Figure 4.5, we ask that you respond to the following three statements:

1. On the NELTA, the domains in which 100% of my actions are perfectly congruent with the "best practices" of exemplary literacy professionals teaching at the same grade level as I teach:

2. The domains in which 50% or 0% of my actions are congruent with the "best practices" of exemplary literacy professionals teaching at the same grade level as I teach:

3. For each domain listed in #2, above, please list the domain below. Next to it write the grade level(s) of the practices that you indicated that you regularly utilize. For example, if you are a fourth-grade teacher whose responses to NELTA questions 3 and 4 were "a" and "c," you would write "Domain 2 (Motivation) preschool and first grade" (for answers "a" and "c," respectively). Perform the same exercise for each domain not exhibiting a "100%" rating on your own personal NELTA tabulation.

NEXT STEPS

Before you read the subsequent chapters of this book, we would like to recommend some courses of action that could be advantageous to you. While we hope that you will read all of the pages in this volume, we also realize that your life is a busy one, one likely filled with numerous professional and family responsibilities.

As such, if you opt not to read the entire book, we believe that you would be best served by taking the following approach to the reading of the next six chapters. Beginning with Chapter 5 and continuing through Chapter 10, each domain is presented in its sequential order, that is, Chapter 5 will focus on Domain 1 ("Dominant Teaching Roles, Responsibilities, and Talents"), Chapter 6 on Domain 2 ("Motivation"), and so on.

We suggest that you minimally do a *careful* reading of one, two, or three sections of each of these chapters. If you are a preschool teacher and both of your responses on that domain (Domain 1) were responses of "a" (preschool responses), then you may wish to read only the preschool section of that chapter.

In this same example, if you gave an answer of "a" (preschool) to one of the domain's two questions and "c" (first grade) to the other item, then we recommend that you do a careful reading of the descriptions for preschool and first grade that are contained in that chapter. If you are a preschool teacher and neither of your responses was congruent with the predominant practice of exemplary literacy teachers at that grade level, we recommend that you read the sections of the chapter pertaining to your first answer (e.g., kindergarten), your second response (e.g., third grade), as well as the level at which you presently teach (preschool).

Such an approach throughout will not only save you time but also enable you to focus upon your present teaching skills. The information in these sections will give you significant information about how you teach literacy and why some of your actions may be better suited to a grade higher or lower than the one you are currently teaching.

Reading about the "best practices" of outstanding literacy teachers at your grade level, even if neither of your responses in that domain was an answer correctly associated with it, will give you valuable information as to what these exemplary teachers do to provide meaningful instruction to students. Its content can also be used as you compare what you do and what they do as literacy teachers.

If, in Figure 4.4, you found that your highest number of responses were most apt for a grade-level other than the one at which you presently teach, we invite you in Chapters 5–10 to read the description about that grade even if neither of your responses in that domain were associated with the grade. As we will discuss in Chapter 11, you may find that all that is keeping you from becoming an exemplary literacy teacher is a different grade assignment. Throughout Chapters 5–10 many figures appear that describe grade-specific exemplary teaching behaviors. If you desire to improve in any of the actions that are reported as exemplary for grade levels other than your own, you can do so by adapting them to meet the conditions needed for maximum literacy learning by students at your grade level. For example, if you are a second-grade teacher who desires to improve your abilities to perform think-alouds, you could use the actions in Figure 10.1 by altering the format and eliminating the large group activity that begins that lesson. As you will learn in Chapter 5, second grade students learn best from think-alouds that are performed when they meet with you alone and because they need frequent, individualized demonstrations that cannot be performed well in a large-group instructional setting.

Above all, as you read Chapters 5–10, keep an open mind. Read about how these outstanding teachers act as they provide literacy instruction to students. Tolstoy once said, "Everyone dreams of changing humanity, but no one dreams of changing himself." Chapters 5–10 can be the launching pad for initiating the significant change about which Tolstoy spoke. As we begin, you can refer to the grade-level equivalents that corresponded to your answers to questions 1 and 2 on NELTA. These questions assessed your present preferred dominant role as a literacy teacher.

DOMINANT TEACHING ROLES, RESPONSIBILITIES, AND TALENTS

Let him teach others who himself excels.

—WILLIAM POPE (1866)

Excellence is an art, for we are what we repeatedly do. Excellence, then, is not an act, but a habit.

—ARISTOTLE (350 B.C.)

We never want to overlook the obvious about exemplary teachers. They demonstrate the quality of *excellence* in every action they perform. The overarching talent that expert teachers in our study possessed was the pursuit of excellence both in what they and their students do. No matter what grade level you may teach, if you wanted to determine what teacher who works with you at that grade level is exemplary, that person would be described in the same way by his or her principal, colleagues, and the parents of his or her students: "Mr. or Ms. so and so is an *excellent* teacher!"

Outstanding literacy teachers realize that they make mistakes, but they are also keenly aware of the consequences of their every action. They know that giving only 99.9%, instead of 100%, every day could mean statistically that one child in every fourth class they lead might not learn how to read on grade level. Decreasing by only one-tenth of one percent the effective execution of our teaching responsibilities, over a year's time, would be equivalent to performing 291 pacemaker operations incorrectly in the United States in a year, writing 20,000 prescriptions incorrectly, or placing 114,500 pairs of shoes in boxes with a mismatched size to be sold in a business. Such decreased effectiveness is more likely to occur if students need to be motivated, retaught, and guided in ways that are not normally employed by their teacher. Since one of our major objectives in this volume is to determine the grade level for which your present talents are best suited, we have placed this discussion of the dominant teaching roles, responsibilities and talents of exemplary literacy teachers first in order of priority.

Our study found that literacy teachers become exemplary largely through their

35

own efforts. This chapter is designed to assist you in reaching such a level in your class-room leadership responsibilities. Although you are likely to be called upon to perform all of the roles that will be discussed in this chapter, you are likely to reach the highest level of expertise when you are working with students whose literacy skill levels best match the dominant role that you most enjoy performing. By referring back to Chapter 4, you can have a clearer idea of the role that you valued in the teaching of literacy. After doing this, you can determine how well your present assessment of your responsibilities matches those that teachers who are judged to be the best at your grade level have identified as being important to their success. If the role most necessary for your students to attain high levels of literacy performance does not match the responsibilities that you most enjoy performing, you could devote attention designed to increase your abilities in the areas where there are disparities between the two. Or, you may decide that a different grade level placement might bring you more professional satisfaction and greater opportunities to attain literacy success for greater numbers of students.

The dominant role that every teacher preferred to perform in her classroom was significantly different by grade level. *Dominant role* can be defined as "the responsibilities and actions that teachers most frequently assume during literacy instruction." These responsibilities, roles, and talents are components of the teaching repertoires that these individuals employ each day during literacy instruction. While excellent teachers were observed using each set of responsibilities described in this chapter to some degree, the traits that were called upon most frequently, and were used most effectively by them, to meet the specific literacy needs for children at an individual grade level are described next.

The immediate response to unforeseen literacy situations is what determines one's dominant role as a teacher. This reaction is shaped by the professional values and philosophy that a person has formed. For example, an excellent fourth-grade literacy teacher approaches difficulties with students' speaking patterns and mannerisms through the strategies used by a coach or mentor. This overarching demeanor is what enables excellent fourth-grade literacy teachers to relate to more of their students than teachers who would approach such difficulties from the perspective of a guardian or manager, for instance. As you read the subsequent descriptors of the most efficacious dominant roles of exemplary teachers at each grade level, we ask you to reflect upon the types of responsibilities that you most enjoy embracing during literacy instruction.

Our research also showed that the majority of highly effective literacy teachers not only frequently display dominant roles appropriate to a particular grade level but also exhibit a high degree of expertise in the way they exercise their responsibilities, talents, and goals for children, regardless of the children's proficiency. These grade-specific talents range from the ability to use sensory-based explanations to stimulating students' deep level of understanding about vast amounts of content. Seven grade-specific roles were repeatedly demonstrated by exemplary teachers during the majority of the time that they directed literacy instruction in grades preschool through grade 5.

These dominant roles were similar to but more specific than the roles that had been identified in prior years by the Praxis Teaching Model presented in the *Complete Teacher Academy: Preparing Tomorrow's Teachers Today* (Ohio State Department of Education, 1990). These dominant roles are presently being used to assess teachers in Ohio as well as for the National Board Certified Teachers evaluation process. In the remainder of this chapter we will present these dominant roles of excellent teachers at each of these grade levels.

This information will be presented on a grade-by-grade basis. In addition, we will also report one of the most frequently cited needs that students at each grade level voiced that they wanted from their teachers at that grade level.

We are including in this book comments from "our consumers"—because if you identified the dominant responsibilities that you perform in your class to be different from those identified by exemplary literacy teachers, reading the following portraits may help to clarify the distinctions between what you do and what students at your grade level most need.

Before you read these grade-specific data, we think it is important to report one other finding of our research. The most important characteristic of exemplary fourth-grade literacy teachers was their ability to perform as their dominant role the one that their students needed at this particular stage in their reading development. Kindergarten and second-grade teachers were the least likely to need to perform only a single role, indicating that the personalities and talents needed at these two grade levels, while distinct, can be executed in a wider variety of manners than is demanded at grades 3 and 4, preschool, grade 5, and grade 1.

PRESCHOOL

Dominant Teaching Roles, Responsibilities, and Talents: GUIDERS

The dominant teaching role, responsibilities, and talents of exemplary preschool teachers are those of a *Guider*. In their instruction these educators build students' confidence to discover print in a manner that is akin to other types of vocational guides (e.g., using teaching techniques that are used by zoo hosts, craft mentors, and museum docents). Guiders welcome parents as active and meaningful participants in their children's literacy experiences. They model how parents can provide continuous literacy learning throughout the after-school hours. They make contact with their students' family members in several ways, for example, making home visits and modeling various family literacy activities to be undertaken by the students with their caregivers. Guiders encourage a child's family members to be involved in literacy activities each and every day, and—more so than teachers at higher grade levels—they try to ensure that this actually happens.

For example, preschool Guiders are masters at responding positively to student inquiries, and they do so more readily and often than their counterparts do at other grade levels. For instance, if an exemplary preschool teacher's class were to stop during a field trip to examine a butterfly, the Guider would be less likely to connect that experience immediately to literacy (as an exemplary first-grade teacher might do). Rather, the Guider at this grade level would most typically be concerned about stimulating and building the children's fascination with nature (and their discovery of knowledge through sight and touch) and reinforcing their proclivities for exploration. Guiders would use such opportunistic teachable moments to focus on developing *oral* language. If the butterfly were still on the preschoolers' minds when the class met later for a shared reading, Guiders might then link this experience to literacy instruction in such ways as writing words that children requested (reinforcing the value of visual input to

Ms. Bonatello demonstrates her role as a Guider for her preschoolers. She builds their confidence in discovering concepts about print by rewarding their curiosity in discovering information about real objects in their classroom.

gain information), singing wordplay games with the word "butterfly" or "b" in the songs (auditory input sources), and touching objects of nature where butterflies landed that were carried back to the classroom (kinesthetic and tactile input).

What Students Have to Say about Exemplary Literacy Teachers at the Preschool Level

"Miss T brings fun things to class. She tells us good things about them."—Rose Marie, a preschool student in Pennsylvania

KINDERGARTEN

Dominant Teaching Roles, Responsibilities, and Talents: GUARDIANS

Guardians is the role that exemplary kindergarten teachers most often assume. They are Guardians of children's discoveries about print, and they cherish students' first attempts to read, however feeble these may be. Guardians are highly skilled at using daily observations rather than printed texts to guide their instruction. These professionals refer to and teach, directly or implicitly. Exemplary kindergarten literacy professionals are exceptionally talented in teaching exactly what a class and individuals are ready to learn.

For example, when kindergarten teachers are performing as Guardians they give directions by stating each oral instruction in an easy-to-follow, step-by-step manner. When they share books, they set an enchanting stage and present exciting literacy skill developmental activities to the delight of their enraptured young audiences. When a portion of a book shared with the group is unfamiliar, Guardians stop and rephrase the confusing aspect of the story or create an example from students' life experiences, to eliminate the source of the confusion rather than simply continuing to share the book. In this manner, the majority of the children feel that they have caught the meaning, and the teacher celebrates this accomplishment. Since exemplary teachers at this level cherish student insights, most children get a good grasp of a book's content and some general concepts about print during their first exposure to a book.

What Students Have to Say about Exemplary Literacy Teachers at the Kindergarten Level

"Ms. M never forgets to have story time every day. She also helps us by pointing to the words in the big book as she reads. And, when she is trying to teach and it gets real hard, she acts it out or makes what she's trying to teach into a story."—Erica, a kindergarten student in Florida

Ms. Howard demonstrates her role as a Guardian for her kindergartners. She delights in their fascination about words and books, and she treats each of their inquiries about print with respect and delight.

FIRST GRADE

Dominant Teaching Roles, Responsibilities, and Talents: ENCOURAGERS

Encouragers and Supporters are the two dominant roles performed most frequently by exemplary first-grade teachers. Our research found that these professionals differ from their counterparts at other grade levels in that they teach literacy all day, and answer questions, irrespective of how seemingly trivial, immediately when asked. Figure 5.1 describes actions you can take to develop these abilities.

Exemplary first-grade teachers also use many forms of student literacy assessments. For example, in their role as Encouragers they make detailed and individualized records for all of their students (e.g., maintain personalized lists of books read, fluency rates, number of sight words mastered, independent reading levels, and number of concepts of print, phonemic awareness, and phonics mastered.) They are masterful in encouraging and supporting while they teach literacy skills. Encouragers do not prompt the use of particular literacy independence skills at a particular moment to the entire class so much as they assist single students in choosing appropriate skills in the process of performing a literacy task.

When you step inside Encouragers' classrooms, you will witness how much the teachers' instruction is formed by developmentally appropriate practice, and how they constantly seek new practices to enhance the print-rich curricula they are responsible for providing. (It is also clear that the teachers are selecting new practices that are based in solid research.) They teach literacy all day, integrated effortlessly with every activity. They hold students to high expectations, including having to read more than one book and to write more than one final multiple-page composition each week.

What Students Have to Say about Exemplary Literacy Teachers at the First-Grade Level

"My teacher does whatever it takes to teach me to read."—Tiffany, a first-grade student from Georgia

Ms. Williams demonstrates her role as an Encourager and Supporter for her first graders. During this lesson, she encouraged Raymond (at left) to read the first word in the sentence on the page, supported Demetria's tracking of print by running her hand beneath the words as she read, and encouraged Chad's oral recitation of the repeated phrases by chiming in with him as he read. Because she encouraged and supported each student—at each student's level of ability—all were deeply engaged in reading.

FIGURE 5.1. Checklist to Assess Whether Teachers Are Assisting Students in Applying Comprehension and Decoding Strategies Independently

❑ *Asked students to explain how they successfully comprehended and decoded* (e.g., After a student read a word correctly, the teacher said: "You just read 'school' correctly. How did you know that word?").

❑ *Allowed up to (but usually not more than) six students to express their answers to questions* (e.g., "Why do you think this author picked this title?"). Then, asked a student to summarize the group's thinking before moving on.

❑ *Often gave students a choice to contribute or not to contribute during discussions* (e.g., "Do you want to pass, think about it for a minute, or 'call a friend' for a clue?"). When the teacher judged that a student knew an answer but needed a few moments to recall it, a statement similar to the following was made: "Let's give Brian a moment to write, and when he is finished we will move on." [Silence.] As soon as Brian had finished writing a note on his paper, Brian said, "OK," and this was the signal that the discussion was ready to move on. Brian knew that the time to formulate his ideas was important, important enough to hold the class in pause for a moment.

❑ *When a student raised a hand first in a discussion, the teacher rewarded that student's rapid thinking while increasing other pupils' time for reflection* by saying: "Great, [student's name]! That is one idea that is ready to be shared! As we give others a little more time to think, can you improve upon your idea and how you want to say it?"

❑ *Did not allow students to "piggy back" on someone else's comments without thinking. As a result, students did not repeat the same concept over and over during classroom discussions.* For example, "Now, we are all stating sports ideas, so we know that we can add any sport we want to our stories. You can write, 'they played football,' 'they played soccer,' and so forth. So, it's time to change our thinking. What other topics do you want in our stories?"

❑ *Whenever a student gave a partially correct answer, teachers rewarded that student and enabled her to learn which aspects of the answer were correct by immediately turning to the group and saying, "Tell me what [the student's name] did right in her thinking to come to that answer."*

❑ *Whenever students noticed a discrepancy between their own and other students' abilities, the teacher stated that the differences they observed occurred because someone had had less practice with the concept to be learned* and not that some were less able than others. The teacher assured all that after this child practiced, the skill would be mastered.

❑ *Usually, the teacher did not begin reading response sessions by posing his own question to students.* The teacher waited after an oral or silent reading experience and allowed students to be the first to make comments or ask questions about the material read. If no comments were made, the teacher would ask questions that enabled students to initiate their own relationships to the reading (e.g., "What question do you think that I would ask about this book? Why?"; or "Which word in this list on the board do you know, and how do you know it?"

SECOND GRADE

Dominant Teaching Roles, Responsibilities, and Talents: DEMONSTRATORS

Demonstrators is the dominant role of exemplary second-grade teachers. These professionals help students utilize their meager or massive prior knowledge bases by demonstrating literacy processes in action. Demonstrations by an adult are more effective than merely restating the instructions of how to do an individual skill to students at this stage of literacy development. The goal of every lesson is for these teachers to stimulate and allow students to extend themselves to learn more literacy.

When you observe a second-grade teacher with expertise as a Demonstrator, you will see and hear her use of many short examples and explanations, continuously throughout the day. In their literacy teaching, Demonstrators depend on their abilities to be creative instantly. Exemplary second-grade teachers seem to be able to formulate an effective and novel approach to demonstrate a confusing literacy concept on the spot, when students become confused or frustrated while reading. Within their classrooms these teachers often, when confronted with a mistake, ask students how best to correct it.

What Students Have to Say about Exemplary Literacy Teachers at the Second-Grade Level

"She truly teaches. She doesn't just give instructions. She tells what she's thinking while she reads. I feel like I can see inside her mind. I want my mind to work like hers."—Juanita, a second-grade student in Arizona

Ms. Stevens demonstrates her role as a Demonstrator for her second graders. She not only brought the life cycle chart to the classroom for the story *The Butterfly* (Palaco, 2002), which the students were going to read, but she provided each student with a feather-light butterfly model to hold. After describing how the light weight of the butterfly will play a key role in understanding the book they are about to read, she demonstrated how butterflies change their life forms several times, another concept that students would need to understand before they read.

All these demonstrations and instructions were accomplished in only 10 minutes, and the students were so excited to read that they finished the book and wrote their own inferences about why the book had been named *The Butterfly* before the class ended that day.

THIRD GRADE

Dominant Teaching Roles, Responsibilities, and Talents: MANAGERS

Managers is the dominant role assumed by exemplary literacy teachers of third-grade students. Managers demonstrate exceptional talent in working with varied groups and multilevel materials simultaneously. These teachers show exceptional expertise in making transitions and in bridging the gap from learning to read to reading to learn. They base their efforts on fully comprehending that grade 3 may be the final year that many students will really have to learn to read. Exemplary literacy teachers realize that many of their counterparts beyond this grade view literacy instruction as a tool with which to learn. With this in mind, excellent third-grade teachers ground their instruction in providing ways that their students can gather information from text. They also help students develop strategies designed to transfer their reading skills to content areas.

As Managers, these exemplary teachers show their students how to make the transition from picture to chapter books. They do their best to accommodate individual learning styles and needs in their instruction. These teachers enable third graders to close the gap between early (basic) and advanced literacy skills so that their students can become better readers as they move from "little kid to big kid" mentalities. In their

Ms. Rodriguez demonstrates her role as a Manager for her third graders. She is exceptionally skilled in creating effective grouping systems in which many students stay continuously engaged in literacy learning even when she is not directing the group. As shown above, Ms. Rodriguez is teaching three students, and at the same time two pupils are working together, one is reading alone, and three are composing a book to be read to the class at the end of the period.

role as Managers these exemplary teachers build on students' varied backgrounds by drawing on multileveled materials. In other words, they locate material that enables students to read words with enough substance to draw their minds into the authors' purposes, points of view, and content. They have a passion and love for bringing the written word to life. Exemplary teachers at this level have great skill in making students feel as though all things are possible. They insert personal touches into their teaching, and since they are gifted Managers, these professionals are able to deftly guide each third grader proactively as a whole person.

Our research investigation also found excellent teachers at this grade level to be masterful at planning and presenting a variety of learning activities that are implemented simultaneously and are well organized. They are additionally adept at juggling a packed curriculum. However, they use time efficiently to work with a variety of ability levels and incorporate multilevel reading, knowing that not all students learn in the same way. Among all the grade levels studied, these teachers were shown to be among the most able users of flexible guided-reading groups.

What Students Have to Say about Exemplary Literacy Teachers at the Third-Grade Level

"Mr. K let us work in so many different groups. I was helping someone this morning and felt good about myself because I had read and helped someone too. I used to not read that much, but in Mr. K's room I read all the time. In the afternoon I get to read the hardest book I can and learn what makes it so hard for me, because I work in all kinds of different groups or with Mr. K."—Linda, a third-grade student in Colorado

FOURTH GRADE

Dominant Teaching Roles, Responsibilities, and Talents: COACHES

> One of the things that I do that contributes to my students' literacy growth at the fourth-grade level is collaboration. We work together more than they ever have in the primary grades. We're a bunch of learners. We are one large and many small teams supporting each other. It isn't just each student working individually in our room. For instance, I cry *every* time I read *Stone Fox*. I suppose it's good to see the power that a good story has on an adult and it's OK to cry. I don't cry to "model" how to really get into a book. I cry because I am really feeling the book that I am reading."
>
> —EXEMPLARY FOURTH-GRADE TEACHER

We have included this quote from a truly outstanding literacy teacher because her words epitomize the concept of *Coaches*, the dominant role and manner in which exemplary fourth-grade teachers carry out their literacy responsibilities. They motivate their students in varied ways while teaching a lesson. Coaches at this grade level are especially skillful in their abilities to effectively teach students how to extract information from a textbook, to apply strategies beyond literature to content areas, and to employ comprehension strategies in science and social studies that entail the use of high levels of critical thinking.

The most distinguishing quality of excellent fourth-grade teachers, in their role as Coaches, is their ability to instruct numerous students of diverse literacy abilities simultaneously during the same lesson (i.e., to aid those who are still learning to read, to push those reading to learn, to teach new strategies to those who want to pull more in-

Ms. Capua demonstrates her role as a Coach for her fourth graders. She is exceptionally skilled at assisting students in becoming responsible for their own growth in literacy. She does so by providing immediate, personalized mini-lessons as soon as individual students reach an obstacle in a text that hampers their decoding, comprehension, or fluency.

formation from the text and use higher-level thinking skills with content area texts, and to establish longer-term projects for those ready to become experts in a particular subject). They achieve these objectives by giving assignments that have differentiated goals, by providing a wide range of books that can be read by students, and by varying the amounts of time required for the students to complete their various literacy lessons. In other words, they coach students to assume the primary responsibility for their own learning, yet these teachers continuously challenge and instruct students to increase their reading powers.

Coaches challenge individuals by engaging them in longer-term literacy projects than were assigned in lower grades. They are also able to empower students to model literacy for peers in ways that result in significant literacy growth for both the instructor and the classmates. They support individual students by making available a wide diversity of books that appeal to a wide range of student interests. Their goal is to provide books that all students can read independently. Walking into an exemplary fourth-grade classroom is akin to visiting a large artist's studio, with the maestro mentoring project groups or individuals with an adeptness that is unmatched at other grade levels. For instance, when you watch a Coach teach a literacy lesson, you would likely observe him instructing students in such activities as how to improve study skills, learning vocabulary words from content books, and doing research and finding reference materials in only a few minutes. The scope of the typical fourth-grade curriculum and the vast amount of content and far-reaching student needs require that exemplary fourth-grade teachers capitalize upon teachable moments in a highly effective manner.

The Coaches' ability to advance students' individuated learning habits was the most important contribution to exemplary literacy teachers' success at this grade level. Also, our research suggested that the dominant role that teachers assume at this grade level, namely, to be coach-like in their approach, contributed positively and significantly to the fourth graders' subsequent literacy success.

What Students Have to Say about Exemplary Literacy Teachers at the Fourth-Grade Level

"Mrs. Nelson lets us check out *three* books from the library any time that we want to. She lets me read them by myself, too."—Deanna, a fourth-grade student in Oregon

FIFTH GRADE

Dominant Teaching Roles, Responsibilities, and Talents: ADAPTORS

Adaptors is the dominant responsibility that exemplary fifth-grade literacy teachers normally embrace. They demonstrate special competence in being able to divide up and teach large amounts of knowledge in learnable chunks so that their students will *want* to learn. These teachers are experts not only in literacy but also in many content areas. They have the skill to provide meaningful instruction encompassing vast amounts of material in a limited time, and they manage to accomplish this in a manner that enables their students to comprehend what was taught.

Adaptors are exceptionally talented in using diverse approaches to bring enthusiasm into the classroom and to inspire students to become interested in the subject matter, whether the topic is the Revolutionary War, astronomy, or decoding. They possess a large quantity of wide-ranging knowledge, and they enjoy and are adept at teaching it in learnable chunks. They use a wide variety of higher-level thinking questions to spur students to attain new levels of comprehension. They also have expertise in developing a parallel focus that is of equal importance—using literacy to develop students' critical thinking and concurrently to increase their self-esteem.

They relate real stories to the curriculum and stimulate students to connect their

Ms. Abdul demonstrates her role as an Adaptor for her fifth graders. She is exceptionally skilled at teaching more than one concept during one reading period and challenging as well as building students' abilities to comprehend at high levels of specificity, abstractness, and criticality. As shown above, students are working diligently to identify the reasons for global warming by combining their work on geography and science, uniting the domains of terrain changes with the effects of the sun and moon on tides and polar cap density.

lives to what is being taught. They are masterful storytellers and dramatists whose classes are fun, active, and exciting. They often teach two subjects during the same period; otherwise, they would not have enough time to reach every content area and literacy goal. They are able to do so successfully because their instruction is carried out in a manner that makes students want to use what they read to produce something new. Highly effective fifth-grade literacy teachers, in their role as Adaptors, not only advocate sensitivity but also regularly demonstrate it. They adroitly vary the amount of time that they spend teaching a concept, allocating anywhere from 15 seconds to several days to it—whatever is warranted by the needs of their students.

What Students Have to Say about Exemplary Literacy Teachers at the Fith-Grade Level

"She varied our class topics so much that sometimes she would just make a humorous comment about something and she asked if we got it, and in a minute we'd learn something and then move on to something else. Or, sometimes she took days to make an abstract idea concrete and easy for us to digest and value."—Tia, a fifth-grade student in California

CHAPTER SIX

MOTIVATION

The level of emotional involvement that students are willing to invest in literacy and the degree of their positive self-concepts affect their motivation to read. Many students' first response to reading failure is to decide not to have a positive attitude toward literacy experiences, become angry with themselves, and/or employ a variety of self-defense mechanisms. They may complain that "Reading is stupid," choosing to make no future commitments to any literacy activities because continuing to make mistakes is too painful for them. Some students declare, "I don't want to read," projecting actions that convey disinterest, since to them such behaviors are preferable to having others discover that they really wish they could read but can't. Still other children may assert that "Reading is sissy stuff," resorting to acting-out in ways that will distract others from observing the negative self-concept that literacy activities arouse within them.

Exemplary literacy teachers know that it is imperative for such students to move from feelings of indifference toward a feeling of total commitment to read—that the unique needs of students at different points on the literacy developmental scale must be addressed. Also, these teachers commit fewer missteps because they are exceptionally talented at intervening when students are faced with decoding obstacles and materials written at elevated levels of difficulty. They know how to stimulate within students at a particular point on the developmental scale, a personal desire for literacy success by varying the breadth or depth of the content, the number of books, the time allotted, the goals, and the variety of materials used in instruction.

In questions 3 and 4 of the NELTA you identified the actions that you most value when attempting to motivate students. In this chapter we want to take the information that you gained about your present strategies and enhance them. The following discussion will present specific actions that have the greatest chance for success with students at different levels of the literacy developmental continuum.

PRESCHOOL

Dominant Motivational Behavior: PATHFINDERS

In their role as *Pathfinders*, exemplary preschool teachers rely on authentic hands-on explorations to energize students' motivations. Their most effective tool is finding ways to relate concepts contained in print to the objects and experiences that students use at home to learn. As expert Guiders, preschool teachers emulate students' home-based activities at school more than do educators at higher grade levels. For example, in studying ducks they use live animals, take field trips to the pond, and participate in learning centers set up with prescription pads, feeding labels, incubators, and records of the number of days until the birth of ducklings inscribed in large-lettered words and numbers mounted above the cage. This frequent and effective use of authentic home-like experiences to teach literacy differentiates preschool teachers from their peers in other grades. The moment an interest is sparked, exemplary preschool teachers are particularly skilled at "running with it." If you were to watch such educators in action, the shift in their instruction would be seamless. The would employ subject matter brought up by the students to achieve their particular literacy goal. For instance, one of our exemplary preschool teachers wanted to teach the nursery rhyme "Baa Baa Black Sheep" so students could sing along with the tape and develop rhyming skills and phonological awareness. As the lesson began, a child said he saw a black bear on television the night before and wanted to sing a song about bears. The teacher said, "Of course." The class sang along with the tape in its original version first; then the teacher put up a picture and wrote the words "bear," "fun," and other concepts on the board. They then sang the song in the form of "Baa Baa Black Bear" and the teacher turned off the volume on the tape at the word "sheep," "wool," and so on as the children sang the bear words in their place.

What Students Have to Say about Exemplary Literacy Teachers at the Preschool Level

"She made me like to read. The books had pop-ups that had words on them and were fun to play with."—Rebecca, a preschool student in New Jersey

KINDERGARTEN

Dominant Motivational Behavior: FUN AGENTS

Exemplary kindergarten teachers are *Fun Agents* who are exceptionally skilled at motivating students by singing; acting out stories, using objects to teach reading, and allowing individual students longer periods of time to develop their interest in literacy learning tasks. They enjoy humor and nonsense verses as long as everyone is being humorous or moving at the same time. For example, they act out silly songs and stories with, and for, students. These expert Fun Agents have exceptional abilities in stimulating children's imagination during shared readings. Each story read aloud is captivating because unique vocalizations are made for sounds and character voices.

Our research also found that these professionals are consistently among the most gifted teachers in their ability to provide time for indifferent students to learn at their own pace during whole-class lessons. For example, students who have not yet learned that print matches speech are allowed to say words aloud; students who do not yet understand that print is to be read from left to right sit beside those that do. Also, students who recognize single letters are encouraged to identify as many of them as they can when big books are read in a large group setting.

What Students Have to Say about Exemplary Literacy Teachers at the Kindergarten Level

"Ms. B taught me so good that when I read now I don't even have to look at the books anymore."—Cody, a kindergarten student in Nevada

FIRST GRADE

Dominant Motivational Behavior: STIMULATORS

First-grade exemplary literacy teachers are *Stimulators* who motivate their students by varying the breadth, rate, and depth of lessons. It is common for them to teach up to 20 different skills in a single hour. An example of such a lesson appears in Figure 6.1. These professionals are obviously and genuinely enthusiastic about every child's accomplishments, no matter how large or small. Their day of teaching is packed with a multitude of constant instructional activities done in short segments.

Another important trait of Stimulators is their facility in motivating children by helping them to connect what they have experienced in their lives to the learning of letters, phonological concepts, and sight words. To illustrate, they continuously reinforce phonetic principles in oral and written language situations that arise naturally. They create wordplay, word-sorting, and current events games so that students can better enjoy themselves while learning how to read and write. Planning varied experiences enables the students to see how many different ways into the world of literacy there are and catches them up in a whirlwind of excitement about reading. It also insures that if a child doesn't happen to be stimulated by a particular activity, something that does help him or her won't be long in coming. Exemplary first-grade teachers are more adept at teaching many basic literacy concepts continuously in short segments than are the expert teachers at any other grade level.

Such expert Stimulators instill in each child the love of learning literacy as well as the will and enthusiasm to become lifelong users of language. They are enthusiastic about a child's every accomplishment, no matter how seemingly trivial or small. When motivation is low, they vary the breadth and depth of lessons.

What Students Have to Say about Exemplary Literacy Teachers at the First-Grade Level

"My teacher makes me like reading because she does not read too many boring books. The books she picks are really fun and short."—Roberto, a first-grade student in Florida

FIGURE 6.1. First-Grade Sample Lesson of Teaching 20 Skills in 45 Minutes, Created by Ms. Valerie Campagna

This lesson provides a model that teachers, particularly at the first-grade level, can follow as they develop the skill of answering students' questions immediately and teaching opportunistically.

Objective of this lesson: Ms. Campagna designed this lesson to teach students how to create images as they listen and read. She is an exemplary teacher, and notice how she stops to address and teach to the specific literacy inquiries of her students without losing sight of her main goal for this lesson.

MS. C: Who can read the title of this book?

SUSIE: *The Polar Express.* [Skill 1: reading whole words; Skill 2: recognizing titles of books]

ROBERT: Ms. C, you always tell us to see if we see anything different about this book than other books that we've read this week? I noticed that this is a Caldecott Winner, and we have read two other Caldecott winning books this week. Do you want us to learn what makes a book good? [Skill 3: awareness of likenesses and differences; Skill 4: review the benefits of reading award-winning books]

MS C: Yes, that is something I want you to learn. Just because a book is not a Caldecott Winner does not mean that it isn't a good book, but as Andrea said yesterday, good books are the ones where you can see yourself in them. Today, you are going to learn to picture in your mind what is happening in a story so that you can predict ahead to learn more. To picture in your mind, put pretty words together as if you were drawing the picture they describe. You will do that for me today, and I'll show you how to do it first. [Skill 5: teaching imagery]

MS C: [Read the first paragraph in the book to the class without showing the pictures.] This is what I did to draw the picture in my mind so I could learn what the author meant. When I read that "I lay quietly in my bed," I pictured what my bed looks like with me in it. It is a big bed, with all white covers, four big posts, at each of the four corners, and it is right beside a window. I pictured myself lying very still, with my hands right beside my legs so that I would not rustle any of the sheets. I had no covers over my ears, so they were open wide to hear every sound. I pictured that the window beside my bed was open so I could hear if Santa's sleigh bells rang. Now, I want you to use the pretty words in every story you read in the future to paint pictures as if you were the main character in the story. I want you to picture what you see in your mind as I read the next paragraph.

BARB: Ms. C, what does "rustle" mean? [Skill 6: vocabulary development]

MS C: Rustle means to make noise by moving the sheet and moving around in bed

CLAIRE: How do you spell "sleigh," and doesn't it mean to kill something? [Skills 7 and 8: spelling and homophones]

MS C: That is a great question! There are some words that sound the same but

Used with permission by Ms. Valerie Campagna, teaching in Ottawa, Ontario, Canada.

FIGURE 6.1. *(cont.)*

have different meanings and are spelled differently. [Wrote "slay" and "sleigh" on the board and gave the class a mnemonic to remember the difference between these two words in that she taught when an animal is killed by another animal it is "slayed" and will "lay" on the ground. Sleigh is something you can travel in the snow with because it has two skis on the bottom so it can glide rapidly across the snow.] You can remember the meaning of "sleigh" as an object that has "skis" on the bottom because both words "sleigh" and "skis" contain *i*'s. [Read rest of page 1.]

MS C: What did you see in your mind this time? [Three students gave great answers.]

DARRON: Why is there a train in front of his house? [Skills 9 and 10: prediction and metacognition to describe their comprehension processes]

MS C: I do not know. Yesterday, we learned how to make predictions. Who has a prediction and can tell us what they did to predict? [Three children answered and described how they performed their comprehension processes.][Ms. C read the next page.] Practice imaging what your mind saw from this page. I just loved the sentence, "the snowflakes fell lightly around it" because I can picture my home in New York! It's so true about snow the way the author described it because just the way snow falls it comes down very hard and sometimes it just barely floats.

EDUARDO: Why? [Skill 11: teaching the concept of crystallization of liquid to make snow]

MS C: Think about when it rains—sometimes the raindrops fall so fast and are so big that they even hurt our skin when they touch us; other times the drizzle is so light it feels like butterflies fluttering on our lashes. When the clouds become really, really heavy, the clouds just let all the snow come at once. But, when the clouds have only a little bit of snow in them, they don't want to let the snow go as fast. Also, think about when you are carrying something heavy, you sometimes drop it really fast and hard, but if you carry something light, you just gently lay it down.

FELIX: You know what you just did! You used a simile to teach us, just like the 30 that we wrote Monday! You said it feels like butterflies! [Skill 12: recognition of similes]

MS C: Wow! I am so proud of you. What is another way you can describe something?

GARY: You taught us to describe things when we write by comparing them to living things, like when I was trying to write about my bicycle wheel going flat, I wrote that it was whistling like a blue jay as it let out its air! [Skill 13: review of personification]

MS C: [Read next page.] I've already taught you how to summarize and why it's important to do so. Who can summarize what we have already read and tell us how you created your summary? [Skill 14: review of summarization] [several answers given]

(cont.)

FIGURE 6.1. *(cont.)*

HILLARY: Could I read a page? I did what you told me last night about not stopping after every word and I want you to hear if I'm reading faster and with better 'spressions [*sic*]. [Skills 15 and 16: fluency and modulations during oral reading]

MS C: Of course! [Hillary reads four pages.] Class, tell Hillary what you pictured and what she did in her reading that helped you paint pictures in your mind easily.

CLASS: [Several answers were given, and Hillary was on top of the world. Every image was correct.]

MS C: I want all of you to divide into the pairs you were in during our reading lesson this morning. Read the rest of *The Polar Express* in pairs up to the last page that I have covered so that you cannot see the last picture that the illustrator imaged. When you reach the page I've covered, I want you to write a paragraph that describes the image that you have in your mind. Then read your paragraph to your partner. Both of you can discuss what you did to image what you think the last picture in this book should be. When you finish, bring your books and drawings to me and tell me what your mind did to image. [Skills 17 and 18: practicing silent reading skills and assessment of imagery abilities]

CLASS: [As the class finished in pairs, Ms. C asked them to write all that they had remembered from the story, and to capitalize the first letter of each sentence and each proper noun. She also asked them to write two paragraphs.] [Skills 19 and 20: practicing how to write paragraphs and capitalization skills]

SECOND GRADE

Dominant Motivational Behavior: CONNECTORS

Second-grade exemplary teachers are *Connectors* who demonstrate literacy by tying together its subcomponents into one whole process. They continuously model how much adults enjoy and value literacy. As a result, most second graders who are taught by them come to value it, as well. Our research found that exemplary second-grade teachers, more than exemplary teachers at other grade levels, pause to perform think-alouds—for example, about what they are enjoying about an author's style or the content of what they are reading—as they read to the class. Exemplary second-grade teachers can also be distinguished by the way they use their creativity to inspire less able readers' joy in reading. They fan the sparks of students' natural curiosity to increase the role that reading plays in their lives. They do so by setting a goal to make each day's literacy lesson more exciting than the preceding one.

Figure 6.2 shows additional motivational behaviors that were observed most frequently in the classrooms of an exemplary teacher at this grade level who was nominated in our study.

What Students Have to Say about Exemplary Literacy Teachers at the Second-Grade Level

"I really, really like it when my teacher makes different voices for characters in our stories that she reads to us, and she does it so, so good that I never want our books to end."——Taylor, a second grader in Virginia

FIGURE 6.2. Most Frequently Observed Motivational Behaviors, Used by Ms. Brandi Smith

Directions: The examples below were used by exemplary second-grade teachers to help motivate their students to enjoy reading. These behaviors can be modified to enhance other teachers' ability to stimulate desires to read by connecting unknown concepts to familiar events in students' lives. Second-grade teachers use these connecting behaviors to (1) tie together subcomponents of decoding, comprehension, vocabulary, phonics, phonemic awareness, and fluency strategies into one continuous and enjoyable reading process and (2) inspire students to improve their own reading abilities and rekindle less able readers' joy in reading.

Frequently Used Connecting Behavior: Tying Hands-On Learning to Graphics/Pictures and Words

Whenever one of Ms. Smith's students asks a question, she immediately takes that student (or the class if many express interest in the topic) to find examples of the objects in question. For instance, when a student in our study asked "Why are trees so different?," many students chimed in with other questions, and the entire class went outside for 15 minutes to view as many different types of trees as they could. The next day [setting the goal to make each day more exciting than the day before], all leaves from the trees they observed were laid on tables alongside numerous trade books about botany. Students like Veronica, illustrated below, were to find pictures and terms that described the trees they found. Such hands-on experiences motivated all students in the class to read, write, and share their new information in oral small-group presentations before the class.

Frequently Used Connecting Behavior: Modeling Personal Joys and Gains from Literacy to Stimulate Students' Reading Motivation

Ms. Smith (like other exemplary second-grade teachers in our study) is an exceptionally masterful monitor of individual students' reading behaviors. When a student seemed

FIGURE 6.2. *(cont.)*

bored, she would model how much books enabled her to keep learning, and that reading was not just something that she did in school. For example, when one of her students began to fall behind his peers in reading ability, Ms. Smith brought in the book she was reading at home for her personal enjoyment, which was a book in the *Little House on the Prairie* series. She sat with Chris and read silently from her book as he read from his. After a period of reading, she shared with him the part of the book in which Jack lost his dog in a river. Jack did all he could to find his dog but couldn't locate any trace of him. Jack was left to hope that his trusted pet would somehow find his way home. The dog did! Ms. Smith then related the story about how she had once lost her dog and hoped the same as Jack. She told Chris that she thought that this book was so interesting, and she was so glad that she read it because she found out that other people felt just like she did. Because of this modeling of her own interest in a book and tying the book to her own personal life, Chris wanted to read the book that Ms. Smith was reading.

Frequently Used Connecting Behavior: Stimulating Students' Curiosity

Ms. Smith adds as many learning modalities as she can to each reading experience. This focus on enhancing details stimulates her students' curiosity as to how the objects she brings to class will relate to the reading lesson. To illustrate, when she reads poetry aloud, she will precede the lesson by spending time choosing a selection of music that will add to the poet's meaning in the verses. Ms. Smith's students not only enjoy and relax as they share in the musical rendition, but the poetic experience frees students to voice their own interpretations of the words that were shared. When their peers express interest in the students' views, a stimulating discussion results, and many seek to read other verses by that and other poets.

Frequently Used Connecting Behavior: Adding Creativity to Reading Lessons

When Ms. Smith was asked what she did to motivate her students, she chuckled and stated: "With me, it is that my students are constantly saying: 'What is she going to come up with next!' and I think they are right! Let me tell you what I mean. One day, a student had asked a question: 'What is static electricity?' The next day, I came to school with many cotton socks clinging by static electricity to my dress. I walked in the room as if nothing was wrong and began our opening day procedures. Students began asking me why I had socks all over me. I played into their hands. I acted shocked, and we had the most wonderful lesson, with socks being attached to them and me over and over again as we read about why they stuck!' "

Ms. Smith went on to say that there was an important message that she wanted to deliver to her colleagues who do not think that they are creative and who might find it difficult to plan innovative literacy lessons: "It's so easy for me to be creative because I'm wired that way. I don't think that everyone has to be born creative to become creative. The more a teacher practices being creative, the more creative she or he will become. I want everyone to experience the successes that adding creativity ideas to a lesson can create for their students." There are also a lot of good books in bookstores that can assist in increasing creative for teachers who want to spend a few minutes increasing this important motivational skill.

THIRD GRADE

Dominant Motivational Behavior: PROMOTERS OF BOOKS

In our research exemplary third-grade teachers were found to be *Promoters of Books* who showed exceptional skill in their ability to motivate students by introducing many genres. Generally, from this diverse array of reading materials, students will fall in love with a specific book. Through the aforementioned action, exemplary third-grade Promoters of Books are masters at keeping literacy interesting on a student-by-student basis. They believe that, as individual third graders discover their own favorite book, the individual child's desire to learn how to read more ably will be stimulated. This increased motivation frequently occurs at this level on the literacy developmental scale because students want to gain the ability to understand and enjoy more advanced books about their newly discovered interests. The 24 most popular books that these teachers use to increase their students' motivation appear in Figure 6.3.

Exemplary third-grade teachers work actively to motivate and engage students to keep the excitement of reading alive. They encourage children by helping them realize that they can turn to print to locate answers, even when these learners lack the self-confidence to do so. They are also masters at improvising during oral readings of books, creating dramatic representations of a character in the story. They keep students interested in reading by introducing new authors, stopping at points that leave students curious as to "what's next" in stories, developing more complete character understandings, and expending extra energy toward accomplishing the important objective of keeping reading classes engaging and interesting. Exemplary third-grade literacy teachers are those teachers who most ably express their excitement about reading and bring reading materials to life for members of their class.

Another important objective of these Promoters of Books is introducing students to literacy skills that are crucial to their learning. Since the students are committed to, and trust, these teachers, the children exert extra effort in trying to acquire and successfully use these strategies. Exemplary teachers are also able to capitalize upon unusual turns in events that capture the attention of students.

Students in these classrooms work hard to learn decoding, vocabulary development, comprehension, and fluency strategies because their teachers' have convinced them that such skills are very important. They are willing to expend this extra effort because of their teachers' ability to build their literacy motivation.

What Students Have to Say about Exemplary Literacy Teachers at the Third-Grade Level

"Our class gets to be characters in the books that we read. Mr. Duffy let me be President Lincoln. I was good too, 'cause I had read all about him, even from the encyclopedia and my brother's fifth grade social studies book."—Jeffrey, a third-grader student in Connecticut

FIGURE 6.3. Exemplary Third-Grade Teachers' 2001–2002 Book Selections That Motivate Students to Want to Read

Hey Al by Arthur Yorinks. 1986. New York: Douglas & McIntyre. A Caldecott Award winning book that was used often to teach main ideas to students.

Coolies by Yin. 2001. New York: Philomel Books. 2002 Children's Book Award

Silver Seeds by Paul Paolilli and Dan Brewer. 2001. New York: Viking. 2002 Children's Book Award. Poetry used by exemplary teachers to teach vocabulary.

A Year Down Yonder by Richard Peck. 2000. New York: Clarion. 2001 Newbery Award Winner.

The Stray Dog by Marc Siroont. 2001. New York: Harper. 2002 Caldecott Honor Book. Teaches kindness to K–2 children.

Tuesday by David Wiesner. 1991. New York: Clarion. 1992 Caldecott Winner. Teach inferences to K–2 children.

A Single Shard by Linda Sue Park. 2001. New York: Clarion. 2002 Newbery Award Winner. Teaches kindness and selflessness to grades 3–5 students. Also depicts Korean history.

Carver: A Life in Poems by Marilyn Nelson. 2001. Asheville, NC: Front Street. 2002 Newbery Honor Book. Teaches many values and inspires students to want to read more poetry, autobiographies, and African American histories.

Bud, Not Buddy by Christopher Paul Curtis. 2000. New York: Yearling Books. 2001 Newbery Award Winner. A 10-year-old African American motherless boy seeks his father; readers will find truth, vision, and hope.

Golem by David Wisniewski. 1996. New York: Clarion. 1997 Caldecott Winner. Jewish folktale and history of the persecution of the Jewish race; how humans must remain humble in times of victory and defeat.

Martin's Big Words by Doreen Rappaport. 2001. New York: Hyperion. 2002 Caldecott Honor Book. Outstanding book to introduce young K–3 students to biographies and the power of fighting with words and not fists. Also, one of the books to include a lifeline timeline, additional book references, and website references at the end.

Baloney (Henry P.) by Jon Scieszka and Lane Smith. 2001. New York: Viking. It teaches the importance of imagination when students face difficulties. It also demonstrates what it is like when you are trying to learn to read, and it contains words from 19 languages other than English, written by the author of *The True Story of the Three Little Pigs.*

Enemy Pie by Derek Munson. 2000. San Francisco: Chronicle Books. Describes how to turn enemies into friends by taking the time to get to know them.

Modern Manners for Little Monsters by Wilson Rogers. 1998. New York: Smithmark. Demonstrates how to take the pieces out of a pop-up book so that parents and teachers can assist children in using their imagination and role-play situations in which they can use their manners to be kinder, fairer, and gracious.

Tough Cookie by David Wisniewski. 1999. New York: Lothrop, Lee & Shepard. Compare the content of this story with the next book on the list. It can also be compared to the Dick and Jane books, in which Dick and Jane's mother baked cookies every

(cont.)

FIGURE 6.3. *(cont.)*

week, thereby establishing the ritual of Dick and Jane having cookies and talking to their mother each day when they came home from school (this was circa 1948). Such comparisons assist third graders to deduce changes in societal values.

Baker, Baker Cookie Maker (Cookie Monster is the Baker) by Linda Hayward. 1998. New York: Children's Television Networks. Compare this book to *Tough Cookie* and the *Dick and Jane* series to see the variety of curricula that have been used to teach beginning reading.

Women Who Dared. A Book of Postcards. 1992. San Francisco: Pomegranate Art Books. Can be used to raise the expectations of young girls.

Dear America—The Winter of Red Snow (The Revolutionary War Diary of Abigail Jane Stewart) by Kristiana Gregory. 1996. New York: Scholastic. Explains the war from one woman's perspective and introduces historical fiction and diary writing to students.

Milo and the Magical Stones by Marcus Pfister. 1997. New York: North-South Books. Demonstrates a new format for publishing students books; has two different endings—students can choose which one they want to read.

Mice and Beans by Pam Munoz Ryan. 2001. New York: Scholastic. Depicts values that are traditional in many Hispanic homes.

The Aesop for Children. 1993 (1919). New York: Barnes & Noble. Some 146 fables, each of which can be read in only a few minutes to fill spare moments in the classroom. Excellent for teaching inferencing by asking students to state the moral of each; and students can also write their own contemporary fables about values they want all people to follow in our modern society.

Esperanza Rising by Pam Munoz Ryan. 2000. New York: Scholastic. Jane Addams Peace Association, Children s Book Award. Teaches many values of Native American cultures.

The Midnight Ride of Paul Revere by Henry Wadsworth Longfellow. 2001. New York: Handprint Books. Has letters, maps, and real documents included to demonstrate some of the innovative publishing techniques used to stimulate students' interests in reading nonfictional text.

Holiday Books. Inc. 2000 Series. Eight outstanding books that develop phonemic awareness, phonics, vocabulary fluency, and comprehension through activities that are described in the books. To receive more information, e-mail Dr. Mangieri at *jmangieri@carolina.rr.com.*

FOURTH GRADE

Dominant Motivational Behavior: INVOLVERS

Excellent fourth-grade literacy teachers motivate by varying their instructional statements so that lessons can move up or down the cognitive scale instantly to adapt to students' expressed needs. These master *Involvers* achieve high levels of student engagement through the use of single instructional sentences. They attain this result by skillfully weaving illustrations from the class's prior day's work into lesson introductions.

To achieve a high level of student involvement in literacy, they share many exciting personal examples of literacy activities that result in improvements in their own or classmates' worlds as well as in interest areas outside class.

Outstanding fourth-grade teachers find "teachable moments" and go with them. They base instruction about new concepts on something that pertains to one or more students in the class, and these professionals are experts at keeping students engaged with topics. One of the exemplary teachers in our study said what in many respects could have been said about these professionals as a group: "I say to my students that, wherever they are now, they cannot be satisfied because, wherever that is, it is lower than they will be tomorrow after the next literacy lesson they complete."

What Students Have to Say about Exemplary Literacy Teachers at the Fourth-Grade Level

"Mr. Watkins talked to each of us for as long as 15 minutes all by ourselves, just him and me. He played baseball with us, and he was the coach of our team on the playground at PE."—Darnell, a fourth grader in Michigan

FIFTH GRADE

Dominant Motivational Behavior: PRODUCERS

We found that exemplary fifth-grade literacy teachers motivate students by *Producing* instructional activities by balancing two equally important literacy goals simultaneously. They produce units of study intended to develop within students critical thinking and self-efficacy as readers. They deeply believe that social developmental goals can be reached through literacy, and the intensely personal nature of their lessons significantly increases students' motivation to improve their reading abilities.

Outstanding fifth-grade teachers apply their masterful Producer abilities to motivational issues as well. They are exceptionally sensitive to, and greatly vary, the amount of time that they may spend teaching a concept. Sometimes it will be as little as 15 seconds, sometimes as much as several days—whatever the students' needs warrant. They are able to have this flexibility because they are experts in many content areas, and they use this ability to promote within students the learning of vast amounts of material in a limited time. They are also exceptionally talented in sustaining students' interest by bringing new research findings into lessons, thus increasing the amount of enthusiasm in the classroom and enabling their students to truly "get into the subject matter."

Another facet of Producers' prowess in motivating students is their frequent use of a wide variety of higher-level questions, enabling them to anticipate students' reaction to a book or literacy lesson before their interest significantly diminishes. A list of specific questions that these teachers may ask when engaging in such instruction (and that can be used to increase other fifth-grade teachers' abilities to motivate students) is presented in Figure 6.4.

Exemplary literacy teachers at this grade level relate real stories to the curriculum and stimulate students to relate their lives to the curriculum. They are also masterful storytellers, and their classrooms are fun, active, and exciting. They make them this way by often teaching two subjects simultaneously during the reading period and also by instructing in a manner that students want to emulate when they read so that they too can produce something new or unique.

What Students Have to Say about Exemplary Literacy Teachers at the Fifth-Grade Level

"Mr. Zerbe made me read books that I thought I couldn't read. He asked me to find the answers to tough questions about them, too. He was right—I could read them. Now, I feel that there is no book that I couldn't read."—Diane, a fifth grader in Hawaii

FIGURE 6.4. Questions and Activities That Stimulate Higher Level Thinking

How can you help students to elaborate on a story?

- Does this story remind you of another story you've read? Why? What specific characteristics do they have in common?
- What parts did you like more or less than the last story we read and why? Were there characters that you liked or disliked? Why?
- Why do you suppose that the author created this story? What is a story that you would have written and why?
- Could you give us an example of what you meant when you said _____?

Write in a journal.

Draw a summary.

How can you help students learn to solve problems effectively?

- After having tried _____, what do you need to do next?
- Can you think of another way that a famous person we've studied would have solved this problem if he or she were here?
- What do you do when you come to a difficult word? What do you do when you do not understand the content/context?
- What thinking process did you follow, step-by-step to reach this conclusion?
- How could we go about finding out if this statement is true?
- What helped you most to solve this problem?

Construct a puzzle.

Use illustrations.

(cont.)

FIGURE 6.4. *(cont.)*

How can you help students express their perspectives or how a story makes them feel?

- After reading this story, has your perception or view of _____ changed? Explain.
- You seem to be approaching this issue from _____ perspective. Why did you choose this perspective?
- What might other groups say and what would influence their perspective?
- How could you address the position that _____?
- What is an alternative?

 Create a diagram.

 Make graphs and charts.

How can you help students justify their positions?

- Why is this one better than that one?
- What are your reasons for saying that?
- What did you (or the author) mean by _____?
- You seem to be assuming _____. Why do you take that for granted?
- Why did you base your reasons on _____ rather than _____?

 Design a panel.

 Divide into groups to debate or present as a play.

CHAPTER SEVEN

RETEACHING

It is not surprising that the ability to reteach a concept that students do not readily understand arose as one of the six domains of teaching skills that helped to distinguish highly effective from less successful literacy teachers. What may be surprising is that at every grade the methods used to instruct for a second time varied. The specific methods used by exemplary teachers at their respective grade level are described on the remaining pages of this chapter. In questions 5 and 6 of the NELTA, you can refer back to review the actions you identified as the ones that you most often take to reteach. In this chapter we want to take the information about reteaching that you gained about yourself and enhance it. The following discussion will present specific behaviors that have the greatest chance to enhance students' success at different levels of the developmental continuum when you reteach a concept.

PRESCHOOL

Dominant Reteaching Style: SYNTHESIZERS

We found exemplary preschool teachers to be *Synthesizers* who use children's five senses as a powerful tool in the reteaching of literacy concepts and strategies. These professionals are the group that turned to hands-on manipulation of letters and words as the second instructional strategy whenever students did not learn a literacy concept initially. By teaching in this manner, these professionals seek to relate students' orality directly to print. The third strategy they frequently use to reteach is to reference many input systems in a single lesson. For example, they ask students to mimic instructors' modeled readings, expressions, and emphases used when they read text to them. These teachers' skills in doing so teaches preschoolers the beauty of fluent phrasing and the rhyme/rhythm of English at a very early age.

They place a high value on, and enjoy, teaching lessons that call upon their talents for creating differentiated tones, pitches, and body movements to emphasize the variability, rhyme, and rhythm of the English language, the alphabet, letters, sounds, and words. Thus, the ability to use oral stimuli, voice modulations, sights, sounds, feelings, smells, and tastes is a discriminator between exemplary and less able preschool teachers. This master plays to individual students' dominant learning input systems so that all students can experience a literacy-related learning episode together, regardless of their prior-to-preschool experiences with literacy-related events.

Preschool Synthesizers are also masters at reteaching by employing multiple hands-on experiences within a single lesson in order to help students experience literacy as a whole class. Rarely is only print, sound, smell, movement, taste, or touch used alone as an input system to reteach a literacy concept.

What Students Have to Say about Exemplary Literacy Teachers at the Preschool Level

"Mrs. Hill tells us the sounds of words and teaches me how to say them. I get to paint letters with my fingers in finger paints, too."—Wyatt, a preschooler in Oklahoma

KINDERGARTEN

Dominant Reteaching Style: STRATEGIC REPEATERS

Exemplary kindergarten literacy teachers are termed *Strategic Repeaters* because that is precisely what they do often and well in reteaching literacy skills to children. They allow more time for students to learn by repeating and repeating and repeating instruction until students have learned a concept. Second, they invite many adults into the room to assist when literacy instruction is occurring. Because of the resultant low student-to-adult ratios, teachers, adult volunteers, or highly skilled peers are usually present to assist children until they gain the confidence to read or pretend-read on their own. Many exemplary kindergarten teachers make available certain written forms so that the additional adults and older schoolmates can record information gained from working with individual 5-year-olds on a one-on-one basis. An example of such a form appears in Figure 7.1.

The third strategy that they employ is to use concrete objects. Phonemic awareness activities play an important role in the curriculum. These concepts are retaught by using students' own language, having them say letters and sounds until they can recognize them independently, and using books that the students have heard repeatedly.

All of the aforementioned strategies used by highly effective kindergarten professionals to reteach center on developing students' abilities to listen to, segment, and blend words. Unlike their preschool and first-grade counterparts, however, exemplary kindergarten teachers use the same text and context to reteach. They are the teachers that most often repeat the same literacy experiences with children. They believe that frequent, familiar repetition increases students' background knowledge and generates "ah-ha" connections with print when each individual reaches specific points in the student's literacy development.

What Students Have to Say about Exemplary Literacy Teachers at the Kindergarten Level

"When I get confused Ms. B helps me. She shows me the words until I can say them." —Bryan, a kindergartner in California

FIGURE 7.1. Reteaching Skill Development Chart: Building on Each Student's Literacy Richness

Name _____

	Book or magazine and author	Pages read	Adult, peer, or parent signature	Adult or tutor comment
Monday				
Tuesday				
Wednesday				
Thursday				
Friday				
Saturday				
Sunday				

What did I do this week that good readers do? _____

_____

Tutor's/Parent's Comment: What my child did better as a reader or writer this week was _____

_____

FIRST GRADE

Dominant Reteaching Style: EXPECTATIONISTS

Exemplary first-grade literacy teachers reteach by communicating their high but realistic expectations *continuously*. In their role as *Expectationists,* such teachers expect and insist that all their students work up to their capacities every day. For example, students are expected to identify new words in books that they read. Additionally the teachers review concepts with students using more varied content, books, methods, and contexts than the students are likely to be familiar with. The use of this wide range of materials is one of the major discriminators between the methods employed by first-grade teachers in reteaching as compared to teachers in other grade levels.

A third strategy often used by exemplary first-grade teachers is establishing two objectives for independent literacy practice sessions. For instance, when students begin to read orally to them, these teachers will say, "I am listening to how well you read in phrases like we just did yesterday and how well you think about the meanings of words as you sound them out. I'll ask you to tell me the meanings of words that you are struggling to pronounce." Similarly, when beginning a sustained writing assignment, exemplary first-grade literacy teachers are apt to say, "I will check to see that you capitalize all sentences and end every sentence with a period, exclamation point, or question mark."

These teachers gradually and steadily increase demands each day as the year progresses, using intense scaffolding with children as they use literacy skills and strategies. Students are continuously engaged in learning or practicing their literacy ability rather than in cutting and pasting or teacher-led drills most of the day. Scaffolding occurs effortlessly and with ease. These teachers' success with students provides clear and abundant evidence that through repeated instruction in new contexts first graders can become independent literacy users.

What Students Have to Say about Exemplary Literacy Teachers at the First-Grade Level

"Mrs. Maxwell told me what I did right when I read my stories. She told me to keep doing it too. And now I can do it all the time."—Jayson, a first grader in New York

SECOND GRADE

Dominant Reteaching Style: CREATORS

Highly effective second-grade teachers distinguish themselves as *Creators* by reteaching through the design and implementation of strategies that were not used with students in prior years. These professionals teach students to master previously unlearned literacy skills by using diverse processes that accommodate the wide-ranging learning styles of children. They are very creative and quick on their feet usually capable of improvising new ways to demonstrate and explain the same concept in a fresh way.

Exemplary second-grade literacy teachers are masters at, and depend on, conducting personalized one-to-one conferences to reteach. These one-on-one interactions enable second-grade Creators to relate to students in an individualized manner, providing them with extra time to fill the specific literacy gaps that children have. They hold students' hands as the children find answers to their own questions about literacy. When students do not learn a concept on a first attempt, exemplary second-grade teachers display exceptional talent in expanding the barely emerging literacy knowledge of children by consistently listening with appreciation and reflection. A description of the effective feedback strategies that they often employ appears in Figure 7.2.

By the second grade, an enormous variety of student reading abilities are represented. In order to reach all children, exemplary teachers at this grade level need to be exceptionally skilled in flexibly helping students develop a sense of responsibility and independence, yet must be available to them when they need guidance and assistance individually. They use one-to-one conferences and tutor often. The exemplary teachers we studied use manipulatives, music, graphic organizers, and read-alouds from well-written children's books and poetry to help accomplish this goal. These methods are employed so that children will know that, despite being unsuccessful in earlier years, they can succeed because new decoding and comprehension strategies are available.

What Students Have to Say about Exemplary Literacy Teachers at the Second-Grade Level

"I know Mrs. Schmidt can help people when they are stuck on something."—Amanda, a second grader in Illinois

FIGURE 7.2. Reteaching Skill Development Chart: Effective Feedback Strategies Activity to Develop Your Reteaching Abilities

Suppose a student approaches you during an independent work period and says, "I'm having a lot of trouble. I don't know what to do. How do I do this?" As you read the following range of possible responses, select the one you would use to answer. Place a check mark before it. Pay particular attention to the implicit effect that each response could have on students' attitude toward literacy based on the information in this chapter. After you have selected the feedback statement that you typically provide students, you can compare it to the comment most frequently given by exemplary literacy teachers of second-grade students.

Response 1:

You say to yourself: I'll just tell Joe the answer so he can get back to work. It is important that students stay on-task.

Action you take: [Give answer, without explanation.]

Example: "Just move the parentheses so that they come after the period."

Response 2:

You say to yourself: I'll tell Elena and explain it one more time, in case she's not clear. It is important that students understand.

Action: [Give correct answer, with explanation.]

Example: "To find the main idea, locate the sentence that summarizes all others or tells the most important point."

Response 3:

You say to yourself: Perhaps if I give Bill several ideas or choices, it will help put him on the right track. It is important for students to have choices.

Action you take: [Suggest several possibilities.]

Example: "You can take a look at the workbook and review the different parts of speech, or you might look over the examples we did last Tuesday, or you might try writing each sentence on a separate piece of paper and look at them one at a time instead of while they are together in the paragraph."

Response 4:

You say to yourself: I'll get Carol to think on her own and realize exactly what she needs to do. It is important for students to develop long-term memory of skills and strategies.

Action: [Ask a yes/no or closed-ended question.]

Example: "Did you try the two strategies we discussed yesterday?"

(cont.)

FOURTH GRADE

Dominant Reteaching Style: TUTORS OF THINKING

Exemplary fourth-grade literacy teachers encourage students to ask questions of themselves whenever they have not learned a concept. These professionals are very approachable, and they distinguish themselves from peers at other grade levels by being exceptionally skilled at teaching critical thinking. They reteach by helping students infer as they read, and for their adeptness at all of these abilities they are identified as *Tutors of Thinking*.

Whenever students have not initially learned what was taught, these highly effective professionals instruct them in how they can incorporate several strategies into everything that they read as well as how to think for themselves as they read silently. Outstanding fourth-grade literacy teachers model thinking on a deeper-than-surface level by stressing facets of literacy such as independent reading and comprehension instruction. Learning to think on high levels, under their tutelage, as one fourth-grade student said, "becomes neat and fun." These exemplary teachers are masterful at reteaching inferencing, imagery, and summarization in new ways.

Another strategy of which they are masters is to meld a special challenge, motivation, and stretched reading ability for individual students into lessons. Our research found that excellent teachers at this grade level select books that simultaneously test their students' thinking and ignite a yearning to read and learn more. As master Tutors, they reteach by stretching individuals' capabilities through the assignment of long-term literacy projects, thereby empowering peers to model literacy for their classmates.

What Students Have to Say about Exemplary Literacy Teachers at the Fourth-Grade Level

"Ms. Goddard always asks such good questions that I have to think hard. When I find my answers, I'm so happy and excited. It isn't easy and not all my friends in other classes have to think as hard as I do. I'm glad I have Ms. Goddard."—Courtney, fourth grader in Michigan

FIFTH GRADE

Dominant Reteaching Style: ANALYZERS

Exemplary fifth-grade literacy teachers are exceptionally skillful *Analyzers* who reteach by analyzing a content domain and emphasizing its critical components when students do not initially understand. At this grade, such professionals do not depend only on concrete examples. Highly effective teachers continuously instill in others their love for literacy and distinguished works of literature by teaching students how to analyze a story's structure, predict outcomes in a novel, and use the writing process to express the depths of their thinking about literacy and a wide range of subject matter.

The second strategy that exemplary fifth-grade teachers often use to provide literacy instruction distinguishes them from their counterparts in other grades. They are highly skilled at engaging students in being stimulated by books. This response to literature is fostered because these teachers are able to regularly delve into many layers of meaning during literacy instructional time that students had not previously considered. For example, they are masterful "devil's advocates," debaters, and/or high-level question posers.

Third, our research found that exemplary fifth-grade teachers frequently use writing and self-assessment to reteach literacy concepts. For example, one expert fifth-grade teacher uses "student self-responsibility literacy guides," which ask students to evaluate how well they read each grading period (see Figure 7.3).

What Students Have to Say about Exemplary Literacy Teachers at the Fifth-Grade Level

"Mr. Markam never lets us stop with only one answer. We can't repeat an answer that someone else gives, either. I love the discussions that we have over everything we read—newspaper stories, chapter books, and even our social studies textbook!"
—Erica, a fifth grader in Washington

FIGURE 7.3. Reteaching Skill Development Chart: Student Self-Responsibility Guides

An effective intervention for increasing students' desire to improve their literacy was developed by Elias and Tobias (1990). Self-responsibility charts improve students' study skills and work habits. These guides are used as outlines to follow as teachers analyze each individual's growth in self-selected literacy pursuits.

A sample guide appears here. It is helpful to remind students of the following facts before they write their guides:

1. Start simply to achieve initial success.
2. Old literacy habits take time to modify or to replace with effective strategies.
3. The "other" spaces can be used to write additional goals for this grading period.
4. Internalization and transfer of learning take considerable time; therefore, students should revisit their self-responsibility guides with you at least once each grading period.

Name: _____ Date: _____

Homeroom teacher: _____

Reading specialist: _____

Read the following list. Check the statements that apply to you.

__ Not decoding well
__ Forgeting what I read
__ Coming late to school or class
__ Reading too slow or too fast to comprehend
__ Losing my books or forgeting to bring them
__ Losing my place when I read
__ Not writing complete sentences
__ Not using vivid verbs and precise nouns
__ Rambling when I write or speak
__ Having limited interest in reading and writing
__ Not reading or writing very often to solve problems in life or for personal pleasure

Other _____

Other _____

Books (or topics) I'd like to read: _____

Activities I've enjoyed this week: _____

CHAPTER EIGHT

RELATING TO STUDENTS

Many people enter the teaching profession because they enjoy working with children and adolescents. Exceptional teachers have developed the ability to gain the respect of students while creating relationships with them that lead to high levels of literacy success. The methods they use vary by grade level, as described in this chapter. In your NELTA self testing (previously completed by you in Chapter 3), your present level of skill in this domain (questions 7 and 8) was assessed. You can enhance your relationships with students by emulating some of the practices presented in this chapter.

PRESCHOOL

Dominant Relationship-Building Skill: NURTURERS

In their capacity as *Nurturers*, exemplary preschool literacy teachers lead students to mimic their speech. Students perceive their teachers as friends. The classroom is viewed by children as a second home—with print added. Teachers establish a classroom climate where students' self-esteem is nourished at the same level as it would be in a healthy home environment.

Highly effective preschool teachers' first concern is the whole child's well-being and, when that is assured, take each student through the gate that opens to the world of literacy. They use the children's fascination with nature and their delight in making discoveries through sight and touch to provide a strong base from which they praise and reward the value of successful discovery as well as to build oral vocabulary. They know that the foundation for literacy success is built by guiding children in making individual discoveries rather than by tying all questions to print. For example, excellent preschool literacy professionals do not talk down to students, nor do they pose questions for which their students know that their teacher already knows the answer.

In visits to the classrooms of these teachers, we would never hear them ask, "What is this, that we are having for lunch today [holding up a cracker]?" Instead, they would ask a question for which they do not know the answer, such as "Last night, what did you like best from the packet that I gave your parents or grandparents to read with you? This _____ was my favorite book when I was your age. What part did you like best? My favorite part was _____ because _____. Why did you like your favorite part?"

What Students Have to Say about Exemplary Literacy Teachers at the Preschool Level

"Miss S always watched us; she watched me even in the lunchroom. I'm sometimes scared in there but not when Miss S is there."—Xing, a preschooler in Wisconsin

KINDERGARTEN

Dominant Relationship-Building Skill: RELENTLESS REINFORCERS

Exemplary kindergarten literacy teachers are exceptionally talented at building relationships. They establish them by praising the correct portions of students' answers and also dealing with what was wrong in children's first decoding attempts. They also use their abilities to incorporate real live experiences to enhance children's experiential realms. They are especially adept at employing real-world experiences to develop oral and written language and to bolster students' cultural backgrounds.

Perhaps the most important ability which our research found that distinguishes exemplary kindergarten teachers from their counterparts at other grade levels is their skill as *Relentless Reinforcers*. While not lying, these professionals never say that a student is wrong. They honor every attempt students make to decode and read, even if the children have not yet learned that the orientation and order of letters in words makes a difference in meaning and pronunciation. These professionals constantly celebrate the class's attempts to read as well as the successes. They do not confuse students by pointing out minor differences related to the concept of letter orientation to a student who is not ready to discern the differences between the visual images such as "b" and "d" unless a student's developmental level is sufficiently advanced that he is ready to learn that concept. If a child is not yet ready to learn that concept of print, these exemplary teachers are masters at presenting a different concept of print that can be learned, rather than to merely wait for concepts of print to develop only through exposures to print.

What Students Have to Say about Exemplary Literacy Teachers at the Kindergarten Level

"Ms. Howell tells me what I do right so I can do it right again tomorrow. I never feel bad in Ms. Howell's class."—Danielle, a kindergartner in South Carolina

FIRST GRADE

Dominant Relationship-Building Skill: CHALLENGERS

Exemplary first-grade literacy teachers differ from comparable preschool and kindergarten teachers in that they praise learning while it is in progress. They also are meticulous *Challengers* who point out even the slightest errors in phonological awareness, phonics, vocabulary, decoding, comprehension, and fluency. They do so in a positive way, and students learn to read correctly before literacy errors become habitual. The specific statements and actions that they use are shown in Figure 8.1, and can increase your ability to respond appropriately to students' incorrect answers. In essence, these exemplary teachers praise a small step forward, ask a child to explain how he or she accomplished a specific literacy feat independently, and then challenge that reader to try to perform the next step on the literacy developmental scale. They do so in as few as three sentences spoken to a student as soon as a child asks his teacher to listen to something they want to read to his teacher.

These highly effective professionals also gain students' respect by explicitly teaching children self-regulation. They give children input into decisions about their own learning by asking such questions as "Are you ready to proceed?" We found that in the classrooms of these outstanding teachers self-guided learners are created. They do so because they pause to answer questions about literacy as soon as they are asked. The children have attained this level of competence because these excellent teachers believe that first graders need to be aware of the printed word and that they can construct and decode themselves. This belief, coupled with their skill in praising successes and correcting errors as learning-in-progress, enables their students to develop an independent application of new concepts, on first attempts, more than teachers who do not have these beliefs and/or who do not possess these abilities.

What Students Have to Say about Exemplary Literacy Teachers at the First-Grade Level

"Ms. Nichols told me that she will not let me not learn how to read. She never gives up on me. She is always teaching me 'bout reading. It is fun!"—Reid, a first grader in Kansas

FIGURE 8.1. Relating to Students Skill Development Chart: Handling Students' Incorrect Answers in a Positive Manner

As teachers, it is important to be a model for our students to follow. Our classrooms are filled with students with different personalities and capabilities. That is why it is pertinent to deal with incorrect answers from our students so that they didn't feel embarrassed and hesitant to answer in the future.

- *Think Again* — This strategy is used when a student gives an answer that is *almost* correct, but not quite. By asking the student to "think again," you give an opportunity for thought and a better response.

Example

Miss C: Why did the librarian ask Bridgett to leave her animals at home?
Carlos: Because they were mean to the children in the library.
Miss C: That was a good try Carlos, but did the story talk about the animals being mean?
Carlos: No, it didn't.
Miss C: Let's think about the story again and try again.
Carlos: Because animals aren't supposed to be in the library because they can make a mess and a lot of noise too!
Miss C: That's correct. Great job, Carlos.

- *Give a Relevant Prompt* — This strategy is used to help students understand a question by giving them a piece of information to think about with it.

Example

Miss C: Why do you think that the Native American Indians didn't like the European settlers in America?
[Class is silent]
Miss C: How would you feel if you were an Indian and suddenly a new group of people show up and start taking your land?
Adriana: I would be mad if someone came and took away my toys and my house. I've lived there my whole life!

- *Reword the Question* — There are times that you will ask a question and a student will attempt to answer, but the answer will be vague or not how you intended the question to be answered. By rewording the question, you can ask the same thing you wanted in a way that the students will understand.

Example

Miss C: By raising your hand, who can tell me what your favorite hobby is?
Ethan: Watching television.
Miss C: I like to watch television too, but what do you like to do when the cable is out and you can't play video games? What kinds of things do you do?
Ethan: Oh, you mean like drawing and helping my mom with her scrapbook.

(cont.)

Adapted from example summaries from many exemplary teachers' classroom observations and rewritten with V. R. Campayne. Used with permission.

FIGURE 8.1. *(cont.)*

> Miss C: That's absolutely correct Ethan. Those are hobbies. I love to read and take walks in the park.

- *"Could you expand on your answer for us?"* — There are times when you ask a question and a student partially answers but is on the right track. By asking the student to expand on their answer, you have them rethink their answer and add to it, or to explain what they meant.

Example

> Miss C: What does it mean to be a burden?
> Veronica: It means that you are in the way.
> Miss C: Tell me more Veronica. You're on the right track. Explain what you are thinking.

- *"Remember that. I'm going to return and ask for that again."* — Sometimes, a student will comment in a discussion but you aren't ready to shift gears yet. Have the student remember their thought and let them know you will have them share it when it's time. This prevents you from not allowing the student to have the chance to participate, and allows you to bring the comment in when it's needed most.

Example

> Miss C: [class discussion on how to find main idea] Many authors put the main idea as the first sentence in a paragraph. Yesterday we learned another sentence in a paragraph that often is a main idea statement. Which one was it?
> Reid: The second one.
> Miss C: Authors usually put their most important ideas as the first sentence or as their last sentence. However, the second sentence is also important. Let's talk about what the second sentence does next.

- *"That would have been correct if . . ."* — This strategy should be used when a student tries to answer a question but has the information mixed up. Many times students say the opposite of what you are looking for because they are on the spot. By saying that it would've been correct shows that you are sympathetic to the students' feelings by not saying that he/she is wrong.

Example

> Miss C: Now that everyone is finished reading that section of the story to themselves, who knows what it means to be *in want of* something?
> Debbie: Does it mean that you have everything you need and don't need anything?
> Miss C: That was a good try. That would've been correct if I asked what it means *to* want something. Knowing that, what do you think it mean to be *in want of* something?

- *Give examples and nonexamples of possible solutions* — This strategy is used to teach students to think outside the box and review previous information in a new way.

FIGURE 8.1. *(cont.)*

Example

[Miss C has been watching Khaina carefully the past 2 weeks and has noticed a lack of self-esteem and confidence. Her grades are average, but there is a hunger to do more. Miss C decides to call a meeting with Khaina to discuss the importance of goals and believing that she can reach them.]

Miss C: Khaina, I want you to write down three things that you want to be able to do by the end of this school year, and two things you want to do in your future.

Khaina: Ok, Miss C, I'm finished. What should I do now?

Miss C: I want you to think about your list and tell me the most important one in each list and explain why.

[Miss C and Khaina discuss Khaina's goals of being able to do long division without making a mistake and traveling to Europe. They talk about the goals that Miss C has and the ones that she has completed even when it was difficult.]

Miss C: Now, I am going to ask you a few questions and give you three answer choices to pick from.

Do you believe that you can do anything you want to as long as you try and never give up?
   O Yes
   O A little
   O Not at all

Will you try your hardest to reach the goals we talked about today no matter how hard it may seem?
   O Yes
   O Maybe
   O Probably not

[To Miss C's delight, Khaina made the decision to believe in herself and to try as hard as she can. She made a choice for herself and she wasn't pressured or forced to do something that she didn't want to do.]

SECOND GRADE

Dominant Relationship-Building Skill: <mark>CONFIDENT COMMUNICATORS</mark>

Our research showed that one of the most important abilities of exceptional second-grade literacy teachers is their relationship-building skills, and they do by being *Confident Communicators*. They listen appreciatively and reflectively. This active listening builds student rapport. When providing literacy instruction, they have learned how to avoid the mistake of focusing so much on what they have to *do* to help their students that they don't actively *listen* to them.

Equally important, we found that exemplary second-grade teachers are masters at encouraging children to have substantive conversations, which enhances their students' abilities by enabling them to learn from vocalizing their newly forming literacy concepts. Among the most frequent behaviors they exhibit when performing this facet of literacy is to hold "discovery discussions." By substituting the term "discovery discussions" for "teacher to student conferences," exemplary second-grade teachers communicate through not only their words but also their actions that teachers and students are *partners* in the building of pupils' literacy proficiency. At the second-grade level, one-to-one discovery discussions have been shown to be the only way that some second-grade readers can express the depth of their literacy problems. Steps that you can take to create highly successful discovery discussions appear in Figure 8.2.

Exemplary teachers at this grade level demonstrate another significant talent that helps to build beneficial relationships with their students. It is their adeptness at assisting students in learning and bolstering their comprehension through discussion. Because second graders within a classroom are concurrently reaching vastly different levels of literacy understanding, exemplary teachers are masters at helping *every* student become a fully respected and participating member in classroom conversations. They were observed doing so by moving forward every child's comments relative to materials read with strategies such as the following:

- Asking students how book characters and themes might relate to their own lives.
- Encouraging students to share their own literary voices and life stories.
- Connecting each student's comments to those made by the preceding speaker.
- Helping students learn new skills, with the aim of enabling them to work more independently in the future when they read more complex texts.

Exemplary second-grade teachers use these same skills to help students transfer their literacy skills, with some teacher guidance, to specific content areas.

What Students Have to Say about Exemplary Literacy Teachers at the Second-Grade Level

"I like it when Ms. Peterson and I work together. I feel like I'm the only one in the room, and she listens to every word I say. I tell her about what I don't know real good about reading, and we find a way for me to learn it."—Gracelynn, a second grader in Oregon

FIGURE 8.2. Relating to Students Skill Development Chart:
Discovery Discussions:
Teaching Students the Process of Asking Others for Help

1. Create a chart on which you and *students* can sign up for discovery discussions.
2. Create a folder. in which you can record the information discussed in discovery discussions.
3. Explain to students how to sign up for a discovery discussion. Specify that they can sign up for as many as one every week if they want to discuss new discoveries that they are making about their reading abilities.
4. Hold no more than three discovery discussions a day so you are not depleted of the energy to stay intensely focused on each student's story about his or her reading abilities.
5. Allow students to make the first comment to open the discovery discussion. If they do not, begin with a question. Among the best are:
   - "What have you discovered about your reading (or writing) abilities?"
   - "What are you learning about comprehension?"
   - "What do you want to learn to comprehend more?"
   - "What is bothering you about your reading abilities?"
   - "What can I do to help you learn to read better?"
6. When students share an insight, paraphrase and ask if you heard them accurately. If you have observed that a student has increased comprehension in a specific way, ask if your observation is accurate. Then the student can agree or explain what they believe has contributed to their growth and demonstrate the new process.
7. To become a trusted mentor, you cannot rush from one student to another. Rather, provide your undivided attention to single students intently. The most important section of discovery discussions often occurs at the end. It is at this latter point when many students gain the confidence to risk asking a very important question or sharing an insight about their reading weaknesses. Without discovery discussions, many students will not have the courage or opportunity to describe their weaknesses from their perspective. End by asking:
   - "What would you like to learn the next time we have reading. and why?"
   - "What is your next goal in reading? When will we revisit this goal to see if it has been reached?"
   - "What do you want to do to help you reach it? How long will it take?"
   - "How can I and others help you the most?"
8. Record the date by which the student wants his or her goal to be reached, develop an action plan to reach it by listing methods and providing time to work on the goal, and return to the written plan on or prior to the day the goal was to be reached.

THIRD GRADE

Dominant Relationship-Building Skill: INDIVIDUALIZERS

Exemplary third-grade teachers are exceptionally gifted in expressing their genuine care and interest in *each* of their students' literacy, social, and emotional development. This is why they can be characterized as *Individualizers*. They are very talented at noticing the individual student's moods and attitudes and frequently let students know that they understand what children are asking regardless of how well the children express it. To do this, they engage in effective rephrasing and build their students' abilities to ask questions without qualms or fear. They have special insight into the intrapersonal makeup of each learner as a result of their caring, accepting, and understanding attitudes toward each individual learner's literacy needs. Two methods they use are to have students write down questions they still have after finishing a reading, and having classmates help each other. Doing this, the students pick up on specific strategies other students are using for deriving the meaning of new words from context, and the interaction can help with vocabulary, comprehension, and fluency.

These exemplary teachers take actions daily to move their students toward internalizing positive associations with the experience of reading, and developing independent reading skills and interests in each one. They accomplish this goal by allowing students to read many books in personal interest areas. Our research also suggests that exemplary third-grade literacy teachers use their superior managerial skills to focus on the individual personality of each student. They actively encourage the development of new student interests, which in turn motivates the children to persist and stay positively engaged when facing specific literacy difficulties, encouraging students to frequently ask peers for help. Such teachers are also among the first educators to teach students how to assess their own literacy abilities. One of the methods that they employ often and well is the self-assessment form, an example of which is shown in Figure 8.3. These forms can be personalized by the class and even by the individual child.

What Students Have to Say about Exemplary Literacy Teachers at the Third-Grade Level

"Mrs. Rodgers says it's OK to ask questions. She spends time with me when I'm in a bad mood, even when I don't tell her that I'm in a bad mood."—Luther, a third grader in Virginia

FIGURE 8.3. Relating to Students' Skill Development Chart: A Sample Self-Assessment Form

Directions: Students can complete this assessment at the end of each week or at the end of each grading period. Teachers write all the objectives and literacy processes taught and practiced in class since the last self-assessment form was completed. Students write the specific objectives they need help to learn in the left column and the objectives that they judge that they can perform independently in the right column.

Name: _____ Date: _____

(Place a check mark next to items that apply to you.)

Need specific help with . . .

1. __ Short vowels
2. __ Long words
3. __ Meanings of words
4. __ Remembering what I read
5. __ Recalling what I read yesterday
6. __ Writing longer sentences
7. __ Reading faster
8. __ Other: _____
   _____
   _____
   _____
   _____
   _____
   _____

Describe what you want to learn next week:

   _____
   _____
   _____
   _____
   _____
   _____
   _____
   _____
   _____
   _____

No longer need help with . . .

A. __ The letters of the alphabet
B. __ The sounds of consonants
C. __ "I", "A," "The" and other sight words
D. __ Blending sound of letters together
E. __ Reading "ch," "sh," and "th"
F. __ Meanings of lots of words
G. __ Understanding what I read
H. __ Reading a full book alone
I. __ Spelling
J. __ Handwriting
K. __ How to study
L. __ Concept of words
M. __ Concept of sentences
N. __ Concept of stories
O. __ Writing a sentence
P. __ Reading silently for 5 minutes
Q. __ Reading orally for 1 page without missing a word
R. __ _____
S. __ _____
T. __ _____
U. __ _____
V. __ _____
W. __ _____
X. __ _____
Y. __ _____
Z. __ _____

FOURTH GRADE

Dominant Relationship-Building Skill: OPTIMISTS

Exemplary fourth-grade literacy teachers exhibit special skills in identifying their students' talents rapidly and in planning and implementing lessons that focus on these talents. One method they use to do so is to label individuals as classroom experts in specific literacy strategies. Students frequently teach peers in their areas of expertise. They are *Optimists* who are masterful at transforming students' attitudes about literacy from negative ones to positive ones. They do so by allowing students to read about their individual talent areas and introducing individuals to autobiographies and biographies of others who share each pupil's propensities. They are also successful in accomplishing this radical change in literacy attitudes in part because they have an exceptional ability to recast students' negative impressions and comments in more positive ways. They are able to rechannel negative attitudes toward literacy by means of (1) coaching, (2) showing students how they changed *their own* attitudes, and (3) assisting students with challenging tasks until they are able to demonstrate that they can accomplish them independently, on their own.

These exemplary professionals regularly model and scaffold their instruction, inviting students to share their own ideas and to develop new thoughts by asking questions and volunteering their own viewpoints. They ask thoughtful questions of their students instead of merely repeating directions. They strive to make connections to each individual student's personal experiences. A significant finding of our research was that these teachers are exceptionally kind, approachable, and were exceptionally willing to invest time before or after school hours to relate to students at their own specifically tailored literacy ability level and interest areas.

What Students Have to Say about Exemplary Literacy Teachers at the Fourth-Grade Level

"Ms. C let us do work together. She let us sit by ourselves and not in tables. She let us teach the class sometimes. She let us talk about stuff and tell others about what we did. The last day of school before Christmas holidays I took the book *The Littlest Angel* to her and told her that I couldn't read it and that I wanted to read it to my little sister at Christmas. She sat with me that day until six o'clock until I could read every page. I'll never forget her."—Amy, a fourth grader in Alabama

FIFTH GRADE

Dominant Relationship-Building Skill: HUMORISTS

Exemplary fifth-grade literacy teachers were found to be in touch with students' more impulsive inclinations or proclivities, often employing or relying on their own well-developed sense of humor, to better relate to their students. It is this fortunate ability that caused us to term them *Humorists*. These professionals are adept at working with students who sometimes feel as though they know *everything* about how to read. These teachers are able to cope with a wide range of learning and maturity levels and have the patience to deal equitably and creatively with those students who are determined to learn "outside of the box" (i.e., beyond the usual guidelines). In the classrooms that we visited humor was often a key component in solidifying teachers' close relationships with students. These educators laughed often, both at themselves and the spontaneous events that commonly occurred while conducting literacy instruction with energetic fifth graders.

We also noted that three specific methods were frequently used to build rapport. First, exemplary fifth-grade literacy teachers sometimes assisted students in better understanding the knowledge they had gained by asking them to turn to each other and to describe precisely what they had just learned during a reading lesson (e.g., "turn to each other and state the two words that you have learned and how you learned their meanings"). Second, exemplary teachers often give a summary of the answers that they would have given on a written test that the class had just completed assessing their reading comprehension. Such an action reinforces to students that the test that they just completed was important—and was also doable, with a little bit of thought. Third, exemplary fifth-grade teachers excel at being in constant contact with parents (more so than is true of their less effective peers), and they maintain that contact in ways that encourage closer connections with students.

What Students Have to Say about Exemplary Literacy Teachers at the Fifth-Grade Level

"Mr. Roberts had a head that knew me by heart."—Rusty, a fifth grader in Minnesota

CHAPTER NINE

CLASSROOM QUALITIES

As you walk down the hall of an elementary school, the energy that radiates from exemplary teachers' classrooms can be felt. The joy and success that fills the literacy lessons radiates continuously. Unfortunately, the lack of growth and the boredom in less-than-exemplary classrooms cannot be escaped. Such differences do not just "happen." In those classrooms where positive achievement occurs, it is the result of the hard work and well-crafted abilities of exemplary teachers intent upon establishing an enriched classroom environment that benefits students' literacy development. These abilities are described in this chapter. Before you read on, you may want to review your answers to questions 9 and 10 on the NELTA. These answers identified the actions you most often take now to create an enriched classroom environment to enhance your students' literacy.

PRESCHOOL

Dominant Classroom Quality: ENGAGERS

Exemplary preschool literacy teachers are *Engagers* who rely upon captivating oral stimuli that they fashion daily to create highly effective classrooms. They continually relate students' orality to print through the sensory experiences of smell and taste. They also use movement and the role that it plays in students' cognitive development to accomplish instruction in literacy concepts. Preschool teaching excellence demands that one be able to follow the students' lead instantly when they take the initiative, and exemplary preschool teachers exhibit this skill more consistently than their counterparts at other grade levels. They can perform these tasks because they fill the classroom with hundreds of objects that are changed as soon as they no longer stimulate students' queries.

This ability is supported by the fact that most preschool concepts can be taught with objects that can be readily brought into the preschool classroom. Thus, large amounts of preparation time are not required to preplan teaching curricula, or to bring resources to teach preschool literacy concepts that students request into the classroom. Therefore, exemplary preschool professionals are in a position to more rapidly respond to student initiatives and interests than are their counterparts at higher grade levels.

These educators are also masters at giving children the space to absorb and explore single letters, objects, sounds, smells, tastes, and words in their own time and for as long as they desire.

What Students Have to Say about Exemplary Literacy Teachers at the Preschool Level

"Ms. Johnson brings lots of stuff every day to school, and we get to read about and talk about it. And after we work hard, we get to eat something new."—Nicholas, a preschooler in Pennsylvania

KINDERGARTEN

Dominant Classroom Quality: WRITING PROMOTERS

Our research showed that exemplary kindergarten teachers display exceptional talent in creating classrooms that are inviting, print-rich, and home-like, enabling children to better associate positive emotions with print. Most often, children's writing projects and interests become the centerpieces for the classroom's wall decorations. It is this emphasis upon tying writing to children's interests that led us to characterize these teachers as *Writing Promoters*. By fully implementing this talent within their immediate physical environment, exemplary teachers enable children to closely associate love, care, and positive emotions with their classroom environment.

We found that such kindergarten professionals continuously write notes, messages, words, and signs for students to use in class and at home, and they repeat these messages so often that students become able to rewrite them alone. These teachers are intimately informed about developmentally appropriate practices and are always looking for effective research-based practices to teach phonics and to enhance print-rich curricula. Letters, words, and sentences are taught through phonics and print-rich environments. They teach letters by letting students have concrete experiences with them— for examples, through the use of such practices as lying on the floor to make letters with their bodies, tracing letters in the air, and so on. Their classrooms are filled with charts that were constructed in answer to students' questions. Teachers help children explore, question, and learn concepts of print in animated ways, using puppets and other physical objects.

Exemplary teachers are also comfortable with having many adult assistants in their classrooms. They use these additional persons in the class effectively so that children have assistance immediately at their side during literacy decoding and comprehension lessons. Exemplary kindergarten literacy teachers use adult assistants more frequently than their less effective peers at the same grade level and also more often than exemplary literacy teachers at other grade levels.

What Students Have to Say about Exemplary Literacy Teachers at the Kindergarten Level

"When I get confused when I'm reading, I can either ask Ms. Rio or one of her helpers to help me. They always do."—Juan, a kindergarten student in California

FIRST GRADE

Dominant Classroom Quality: SAFETY NETTERS

Outstanding first-grade literacy teachers create print-rich space for students to explore resources, but unlike the case in prior grades, classrooms and all literacy materials are organized at students' eye level so that students can view them continuously and use them regularly without their teachers prompting them to do so. Exemplary teachers nurture students and instruct with attention to creating the safest possible environment for attempting new literacy feats. It is their regular and effective provision of continuous support that led us to characterize these educators as *Safety Netters*. They manage the instructional pace and classroom routines through lessons that are exceptionally well matched to students' achievement levels. Teachers make use of classroom resources that can assist in reading, writing, and spelling (e.g., easel displays and charts with a large number of words on them). Students' writing is prominently displayed in the room, and when students "publish" their books, they are taught to input the content of them into a computer. Instruction also focuses on wordplay, using daily interactions with print involving tongue twisters, rhymes, and the repeated rereading of easy patterned text; students are encouraged to read along and then write. Some 48 books employing repetitive language (e.g., *Out, Out, Out*) that are used most often by these teachers (and can be used to increase the quality of other first-grade classrooms) are listed in Figure 9.1.

More frequently than in kindergarten, first-grade print-rich environments are designed for students to reach for and use literacy materials independently. Exemplary teachers encourage first graders to come to them and read. By having them engage in this practice, these teachers are also seeking to develop their students' desires to learn more about literacy as well as to reduce their anxiety about reading independently.

What Students Have to Say about Exemplary Literacy Teachers at the First-Grade Level

"Mrs. Kapland helps me when I need help when I'm reading. And when I really don't understand, she stays with me to explain it until I understand it."—Tran, a first grader in Texas

FIGURE 9.1. Building More Effective Classrooms
Skill Development Chart: 48 Predictable Books Used by Exemplary First-Grade Teachers to Build a Print-Rich Environment

Alexander, M. (1968). *Out! Out! Out!* New York: Dial.

Aliki. (1983). *Use your head, dear.* New York: Greenwillow.

Allen, P. (1983). *Who sank the boat?* New York: Coward-McCann.

Ardizzone, E. (1970). *The wrong side of the bed.* New York: Doubleday.

Asch, E. (1988). *Mooncake.* New York: Aladdin.

Borden, L. (1989). *Caps, hats, socks, and mittens: A book about the four seasons.* New York: Scholastic.

Borden, L. (1991). *The watching game.* New York: Scholastic.

Bottner, B. (1987). *Zoo song.* New York: Scholastic.

Brown, D. (1993). *Ruth Low thrills a nation.* New York: Ticknor & Fields.

Brown, M. W. (1947). *Good night moon.* New York: Harper & Row.

Bunting, E. (1990). *The wall.* New York: Clarion.

Burningham, J. (1985). *Slam bang skip trip, sniff shout, wobble pop.* New York: Viking.

Carle, E. (1970). *The very hungry caterpillar.* New York: Hamilton.

Carlson, B. (1982). *Let's find the big idea.* New York: Abingdon Press.

Charlip, R., & Joyner, J. (1994). *Thirteen.* New York: Aladdin.

Christelow, E. (1989). *Five little monkeys jumping on the bed.* New York: Clarion.

Cooper, S. (1983). *The silver cow: A Welsh tale.* New York: McElderry Books.

Crews, D. *School bus.* New York: Greenwillow.

DeSantis, K. (1985). *A doctor's tools.* New York: Dodd.

Delacre, L. (1991). *Nathan's balloon adventure.* New York: Scholastic.

Demarest, C. (1991). *No peas for Nellie.* New York: Aladdin.

Dodd, A. (1994). *Footprints and shadows.* New York: Aladdin.

Faulkner, M. (1991). *The moon clock.* New York: Scholastic.

Fox, M. (1986). *Hattie and the fox.* New York: Bradbury.

Gibbons, G. (1983). *The boat book.* New York: Holiday House.

Ginsbury, M. (1983). *The magic stove.* New York: Coward-McCann.

Greenfield, E. (1981). *Daydreamers.* New York: Dial.

Guarino, D. (1989). *Is your mama a llama?* New York: Scholastic.

Guy, R. (1981). *Mother crocodile: An Uncle Amadou tale from Senegal.* New York: Delacorte.

Gwynne, F. (1990). *A little pigeon toad.* New York: Aladdin.

Hoban, T. (1975). *Dig, drill, dump.* New York: Greenwillow.

Hoban, T. (1984). *I walk and read.* New York: Greenwillow.

FIGURE 9.1. *(cont.)*

Hoban, T. (1989). *More than one.* New York: Greenwillow.

Hopking, L. (1984). *Surprises.* New York: Harper & Row.

Hurwitz, J. (1990). *Busybody Nora.* New York: Morrow.

Hutchins, P. (1968). *Rosie's walk.* New York: Macmillan.

Hutchins, P. (1972). *Rosie's walk.* New York: Weston Woods.

Kingman, L. (1953). *Peter's long walk.* New York: Doubleday.

Kraus, R. (1974). *Owliver.* New York: Windmill.

Louie, A. *Yeh-Shen: A Cinderella story from China.* New York: Philomel.

Maestro, B., & Maestro, G. (1978). *Busy day: A book of action words.* New York: Crown.

Martin, B. ,Jr. (1967). *Brown bear, brown bear, what do you see?* New York: Holt.

Redmond, J. (1993). *Elephant.* New York: Knopf.

Rockwell, H. (1975). *My dentist.* New York: Greenwillow.

Sendak, M. (1963). *Where the wild things are.* New York: Harper & Row.

Shaw, C. (1947). *It looked like spilt milk.* New York: Harper & Row.

Tolstoy, A. (1968). *The great big enormous turnip.* New York: Franklin Watts.

Zemach, M. (1965). *The teeny tiny woman.* New York: Scholastic.

SECOND GRADE

Dominant Classroom Quality: CHALLENGERS

Exemplary second-grade literacy teachers are *Challengers* because they create a positive classroom environment that challenges students to think on a deeper level. Their classroom environments are more relaxed than those found in preschools, kindergartens, or first grades. The resources and print experiences that these professionals provide to their students stimulate them to think about reading independently. Exemplary second-grade teachers' rooms are distinguished from those of less effective peers in that the former are significantly more print-rich. These exemplary teachers visually emphasize diversity in their literacy instruction, and their teaching also demonstrates how students must learn to accept the consequences in determining meaning of making occasional mistakes during reading and writing (and how to overcome these consequences). A visual image you would see of this teaching skill would be teacher-made charts entitled "What to Do When You Don't Know a Word When You Are Reading Alone," and "What You Can Do When You Don't Understand."

Equally important, these teachers are exceedingly adept at bridging the performance gap between students who are still emergent readers and those who are more skill-wise while still managing to keep both groups interested and engaged in literacy-enhancing activities. They integrate reading and writing through learning centers and throughout the entire classroom. They also pair students to read orally to practice decoding and fluency.

What Students Have to Say about Exemplary Literacy Teachers at the Second-Grade Level

"I never think that I can't do anything in my class. Ms. Miller tells me that I can do anything that I want to do, and when I think I can't do something she puts up a chart that I can look at to help me do it until I can do it by myself."—Matthew, a second grader in Florida

THIRD GRADE

Dominant Classroom Quality: ORGANIZERS

Exemplary third-grade teachers are termed *Organizers* because they are masterful in managing a class so that students do lots of reading to themselves and to one another. They often do so by engaging in more author studies than their peers at lower grade levels. A list of such author studies that can be used in the classroom to increase students' engagement appears in Figure 9.2.

Masterful third-grade teachers also use resources that bridge learning to read and reading to learn. As one student stated: "Mr. T put more good stuff up on the bulletin boards to read than any other third-grade teacher in our school."

These educators are also quite adept at rearranging the furniture in their rooms so that they can group students of like capabilities on a moment's notice. For instance, they can organize their classrooms in ways that provide the time that will enable students who need to spend more time with the teacher to learn to read longer books—perhaps their very first chapter books. They proactively use this strategy because not only are they teaching students how to read, but also they are positioning students to explore their interests independently and in groups. An important facet of their expertise is their ability to manage the class so that students have time to think about several types, or genres, of books every day.

What Students Have to Say about Exemplary Literacy Teachers at the Third-Grade Level

"Ms. Waterman teaches us to be very organized. When she teaches reading, she's organized and we learn how to be like her when we read."—Cherie, a third grader in Louisiana

FIGURE 9.2. Building More Effective Classrooms Skills Development Chart: Author Studies That Characterized Expert Teachers' Classrooms

Early elementary school

Eric Carle   *www.eric-carle.com*

Have the students read one of Eric Carle's books and do research on him. The students should then write a story in the same format as Eric Carle or a story that correlates with his content and/or characters. When the students are done, they should have three things to present: (1) a book review, (2) background information on the author, and (3) a completed book.

Norman Bridwell   *www.scholastic.com/clifford/kids/welcome.htm*

Complete a guided reading of *Clifford the Big Red Dog* with the students. Students in a group can talk about the author (Norman Bridwell) and, as a class, discuss how Norman Bridwell writes his books. In groups, younger students can write a short story about an animal that has personification. (Include a discussion of personification for younger students.)

Gene Zion: *Harry the Dirty Dog* books   *my.linkbaton.com/bibliography/zion/gene*

Ask students to write a sequel to a book that has been read.

Elementary school

Stan and Jan Berenstain   *villa.lakes.com/mariska/bears/bio.html*

Have students read one of the Berenstain Bears books. The students should complete an author study about Stan and Jan Berenstain. After the completion of these two activities, have the students draw a cartoon. The cartoon should include characters with a problem; there should be problem-solving tactics, and so on. Length and content should be teacher-specific.

Joanna Cole and Bruce Degen   *www.scholastic.com/magicschoolbus/books/index.htm*

Students should read one of the Magic School Bus books and do an author study of Joanna Cole and Bruce Degen. Prepare any lesson that correlates to the book that has been read. Have the students create another "magic object" and write a short story about it. When the stories are completed, have the students read their stories in the author's chair.

Arnold Lobel: Frog and Toad books   *www.sdcoe.k12.ca.us/score/frog/frogtg.html*

Tomie dePaola   *www.bingley.com/Biography.html*

Chris Van Allsburg   *www.remc8.k12.mi.us/eastgr/rapr/htmls/new/people/*
ewfam.html
www.eduplace.com/rdg/author/cva/classroom.html

Dr. Seuss   *www.randomhouse.com/seussville*

Students compare these authors' writing styles in small groups and report their findings to the class.

Older elementary school–middle school

Jan Brett   *www.janbrett.com*

Have students write a short chapter book. Introduction of lesson should focus on chapter books and how they are used by advanced readers. If having the students read a

FIGURE 9.2. *(cont.)*

chapter book by themselves is too difficult, set some extra time at the end of the day to have a shared reading. Read the book aloud and have students follow along with their own books.

Judy Blume   *www.judyblume.com*

Have students read one of Judy Bloom's books and do research on her. The students should then write a story in the same format as the book they read or a story that resembles typical Judy Blume content and/or characters.

R. L. Stein   *scholastic.com/goosebumps/high/index.htm*

Have the students read one of the Goosebumps books, following the same general guidelines as in the other author studies. Have the students write a mystery book that has some frightening elements. Class discussion should involve creating a mystery and how to add frightening elements. Discuss with the students the appropriate level of horror for their mysteries.

E. B. White: *Stuart Little*   *www.harperchildrens.com/hch/author/author/white*

Roald Dahl: *Matilda* and *James and the Giant Peach*   *www.geocities.com/Hollywood/
                                                            Academy/4613/dahl.html*

Lynn Reid Banks: *The Indian in the Cupboard* and other books   *www.lynnereidbanks.com
                   www.friend.ly.net/scoop/biographies/bankslynne/index.htm*

Madeleine L'Engle: *A Wrinkle in Time*   *the-casteels.com/~castiron/lengle.html*

L. M. Montgomery: Anne of Green Gables books   *www.dd.chalmers.se/~f95lean/
                                                       authors/lmmlink.html*

J. K. Rowling: Harry Potter books   *www.sffworld.com/authors/r/rowling_jk*

William Steig: *Abel's Island*   *www.williamsteig.com*

Divide the class into groups. Students choose the author above they want to research. They read three of the author's books, identify key elements in the author's writing style that they enjoy, and report to the class. After all presentations are complete, students make a class list of qualities in literature that they value.

Middle-school

Sherry Garland   *www.scholastic.com/dearamerica/index.htm*

According to its publishers, the near America books invite you "into the personal experience of girls from different times in American history. The books and television shows are inspired by real letters and diaries from girls who lived in extraordinary circumstances. You will experience firsthand what it was like to grow and live in another time and place. Have students write a letter about what is currently happening in the world. Create a time capsule and have each student contribute something to put into the time capsule. Bury the time capsule in the schoolyard and have a reunion set for the following year, or even later, when students can rediscover their letters.

Ann M. Martin   *www.scholastic.com/annmartin/bsc/index.htm*

Have a class perform the same activities for a Baby-Sitters Club book as in the rest of the author studies. The students should then write a lesson about responsibility. Lead a discussion of responsibility and how to become a responsible student. Use everyday examples and examples that can be applied in the classroom.

FOURTH GRADE

Dominant Classroom Quality: AUTHENTICATORS

Exemplary fourth-grade literacy teachers have classroom environments that complement their use of coaching strategies that serve as *Authenticators* of the real world. They mentor pupils continuously on how to locate resources that will enable them to make important decisions based on the content of the books that they read. These professionals are also the teachers who most often spotlight the timeless issues facing all human beings (e.g., justice, liberty, and truth), and their room decor often reflects such topics. The basic instructional principles of such teachers are to expose students to real-world events and to judiciously guide their students through the welter of confusion. Their goal is to have students make lifelong commitments to reading and to making the world a better place to live. More often than exemplary teachers in grades K–3, these teachers enjoy a classroom in which current events are read about, from more than one source.

An equally important ability of exemplary teachers at this grade level is to personalize instruction in ways that will help students better understand how literacy can help them live a fulfilling and successful life. They achieve their goals by presenting more whole class introductions about new reading strategies than exemplary third- and fifth-grade teachers would. They also teach literacy skills through social studies projects and during social studies class periods.

What Students Have to Say about Exemplary Literacy Teachers at the Fourth-Grade Level

"In Mr. Watkins's classroom, we talk about stuff that is important not just in school but in our country. He gets me to think and read about things that no other teacher got me to think about before."—Levon, a fourth grader in New York

FIFTH GRADE

Dominant Classroom Quality: PLANNERS

Outstanding literacy educators in the fifth grade are exemplary *Planners*. They use their expertise in planning to teach vast amounts of material while stimulating students' deep interest in, and high levels of understanding of, the concepts taught. These individuals are organized, plan often and well, and spend time before each day to ensure that everything is in place so that the day runs smoothly. They don't waste time. Every year they have more content to teach and less time in which to do it. They meet students' needs while providing instruction in content topics that must be taught as well as in current events that spontaneously occur during the school year.

Because of their expertise in planning, they are able to still provide meaningful chunks of time for literacy instruction to occur, despite the many special school-generated activities that take time out of the daily schedule. While they have similar classroom organizations to exemplary third-grade teachers, because exemplary fifth-grade teachers will more frequently have small groups complete projects at different times, these teachers have exceptional skill in impromptu teaching of small groups. These sessions are designed to increase students' ability to specifically document and thoroughly present facts and major concepts from materials read. Thus, when observing such classrooms one views numerous multileveled resource books on shelves, many projects in various stages of completion on tables, and many impromptu reading strategy lessons being delivered to small groups.

What Students Have to Say about Exemplary Literacy Teachers at the Fifth-Grade Level

"Even on days when our school has long assemblies, Mr. Davis makes sure that he still teaches reading to us."—Conrad, a fifth grader in Wisconsin

CHAPTER TEN

LESSON CHARACTERISTICS

Prior to the publication of this book, professors in most colleges and schools of education taught the same lesson plan format to all elementary preservice and graduate-level teachers. It was believed that a standard format would address the needs that all teachers would face regardless of the grade level at which they taught. Data to be presented in this chapter will refute this assumption by showing that unique features should be included in lessons designed for specific grade levels. Our research found that the traits of effective lesson plans developed by outstanding teachers and the assessments used by them varied according to the grade level at which they taught. When the qualities that will be subsequently described were built into literacy lessons, students at the respective grade level increased their reading abilities significantly. Before you read on, you may want to reread the answers that you gave to questions 11 and 12 on the NELTA. These answers identified the characteristics that you normally include in your literacy lessons. In this chapter, we want to take the information that you gained about your lesson plans and improve upon your planning skills. The following discussion will present specific lesson features that have the greatest chance for success with students at different levels on the literacy developmental continuum.

PRESCHOOL

Dominant Lesson-Planning Strategy: CONDUCTORS

Exemplary preschool teachers incorporated certain characteristics into their literacy lessons significantly more frequently than did their less effective peers. These individuals varied the tones, pitches, and body movements that they utilized in the majority of their lessons so that they could more clearly demonstrate visually and kinesthetically the variability, rhyme, and rhythm of English to children. They also sang songs, did chants, and recited poems by using different tones, pitches, and body motions. They acted in such a manner because such actions have been found to be highly effective in helping emergent readers to more readily learn literacy concepts and the alphabet.

Exemplary preschool teachers also assisted students in memorizing poems by asking them to mimic their own modeled speech patterns as they read poems. Because of their heavy reliance on oral exercises and activities in teaching literacy lessons, preschool professionals, of necessity, provide lessons that are rich in oral responsive language modeling. They often ask their students to repeat their modeled speaking and reading patterns as a daily component in literacy development.

Similarly, vocabulary is also built through continual repetition of spoken words in chants, songs, poems, and prose readings. Our research found these lesson characteristics to be crucial elements in preschoolers' desire to want to learn to decipher print. Each time these oral components were reiterated, children were given clear reminders that visual print contained words that could be rendered orally and that words contained letters, a fact that helped them to understand the alphabetic principles of the English language.

In addition, exemplary preschool literacy teachers help children use a wider variety of writing materials than their less effective peers. Exemplary professionals expect that, by age 3, children begin to perceive that undecipherable lines actually contain identifiable letters. It is at this point that these teachers have already helped most of their students to recognize that printed words convey information. While the scribbling of many preschoolers will not resemble real writing, such teachers use these kinesthetic and tactile interactions, coupled with their oral and reading modeling, to pave the way for real decoding and composition activities that may emerge as early as the end of the preschool year.

The exemplary teachers that we studied also develop concepts of print, letters, and sounds through students' listening to children's literature. This facet of their instruction is what these teachers as well as many experts believe is the most important thing that they do to contribute to preschoolers' literacy success.

What Students Have to Say about Exemplary Literacy Teachers at the Preschool Level

"Ms. B doesn't sing real good but teaches us good songs that we love and read all the time."—Emily, a preschooler in North Carolina

KINDERGARTEN

Dominant Lesson-Planning Strategy: POSITIVE PACERS

Exemplary kindergarten teachers are masters at creating lessons that respect and allow for a student's individualized pace of learning. As a result of their belief in their students, positive results usually occur. It is as a result of their blending positive action and individualized pacing that we have termed these teachers *Positive Pacers.*

Research has unveiled an interesting human phenomenon. It is that students, even as young as 5 years of age, will tend to live up to others' expectations of them. When children perceive that their teachers see the best in them, most of them turn their best selves toward their teachers. As a result, under the guardianship of exemplary kindergarten lessons children will engage in significantly more literacy tasks because they want to share more of their best selves with their teachers. The pleasing result is that kindergarten children, through exemplary lessons that contain the following features, have been found to:

- Move their eyes appropriately from left to right as they read print in big books and eventually as they pretend to read smaller books.
- Read the alphabet and individual letters more frequently and learn letter names and sounds faster.
- Play more oral blending games with and without their teachers being present.
- More fully engage in phonemic development activities such as oral segmentation of separate words into sounds.

Like masterful preschool teachers, exemplary kindergarten professionals use individual writing assignments and interactive writing experiences every day. However, what is included in these lessons differs significantly from preschool lessons. Students and teachers write together (e.g., one-to-one instruction during journal writing activities and composing group thank-you letters). Students write what they can, and teachers write the rest. Teachers spell or write words that students request and are also beside the children as they scribble or write letters. This simultaneous oral, written, reading, and listening integration at the word and letter learning stage has been found to contribute significantly to outstanding kindergarten students' subsequent rapid reading development.

What Students Have to Say about Exemplary Literacy Teachers at the Kindergarten Level

"Mr. T's reading lessons are so good that I can read now, and I'm not afraid to sound out new words."—Brandon, a kindergartner in California

FIRST GRADE

Dominant Lesson-Planning Strategy: OPPORTUNISTS

Exemplary first-grade teachers teach literacy all day, as described earlier in this volume. Their individual lessons are rapid-paced and play-filled, and they tell students why and how specific decoding, comprehension, vocabulary, and fluency strategies work when they introduce a concept. These professionals teach lessons in which they can take the opportunity to share in the fun of learning literacy with students opportunistically. For example, when one exemplary teacher introduced how to read two syllable words, she used a leprechaun theme. She asked the students to find the pots of gold that the leprechaun had left outside. Inside each golden bag were 10 word cards related to St. Patrick's Day. Each bag contained different two-syllable words, and the students placed their cards on a large shamrock tree in the room in appropriate slots so the resultant meanings made a class story. The story was then sung by all to the tune of "Old Mac-Donald." For the rest of the day, to review the words, the teacher said, "if we sing the words correctly, the leprechaun may come to see us." At the end of the day every student could read the 200 words in random order, and a parent, dressed as a leprechaun, came to read a book to the class. For their effective use of each of the aforementioned strategies, they are designated as *Opportunists.*

Such professionals additionally teach synthetic phonics (teaching students to decode words by blending single letter sounds), onset-rhyme (teaching students to decode by analyzing initial consonant and vowel-ending patterns separately and blending them together), and spelling strategies, without denying children access to authentic and intrinsically valuable children's literature. Teachers show students how to use their phonemic awareness skills in conjunction with context clues and each new decoding strategy introduced. Our research found that these professionals understand how to implement such a broad-based literacy program better than less effective peers.

Excellent first-grade teachers are also highly effective in integrating reading and writing instruction with every activity. Thematic units drive much of what is read and written by their students. Writing occurs frequently in the context of science and social studies instruction so that students compose twice daily. As a result, students have opportunities to use the skills they are learning throughout the school day. When possible, these teachers seek to keep instruction relevant to students' lives, access their prior knowledge, employ all available literacy resources, use literature in all subjects, and recognize the need to address the multiple uses of literacy.

By the end of the year, there are great demands on most students with respect to grammar. For example, students are taught to check their writing to determine whether the grammatical conventions are correct. Students are taught reading and writing skills every day. In the classrooms of these teachers, this translates frequently in students reading more than one book and writing more than one final product a week. As they plan, draft, and then revise as they read and write, students use resources that are constantly made available by the teacher and that are in the classroom.

One-to-one teacher conferences occur as a part of the revision and small-group reading processes. Editing sheets and cue cards utilized in the writing process are displayed in the classrooms of these exemplary educators. Teachers encourage the use by children of many decoding and comprehension strategies in single lessons. An example of how such lessons are planned appeared in a poem written by one exemplary teacher, which was later published in *The Reading Teacher* (March 2000, Vol. 53, No. 6, p. 515):

Reading à la First Grade

by

Nancy Warmbold Zamor

Oh, the places you'll go, when you've learned to read . . .
Your mind will sprout seedlings from one tiny seed,
That may start with a character, problem, or plot,
That engage you in reading and thinking a lot.

But to get to that wonderful, mind-growing place,
You've got to start *here*, and proceed at a pace
That is steady and sure. Well, you'll move right along
If you gobble up words, you'll grow sturdy and strong.

Start with the pictures that help tell the tale.
Learn some words by heart, and then follow the trail
Of sounds at beginnings, and sounds at the end.
And does it make sense? On that you'll depend!

Go back to the start, try the whole thing once more,
Or spell it out loud, 'til that word starts to roar . . .
And if it still stumps you, refuses to grow,
Then peer deep within it, find one part you know.

And say that one part, and add on a sound
Until it grows bigger, and a new word you've found.
Or take a good guess that will make it make sense
Try all of these things! Let reading commence!
And if *you* have a friend who's just learning to read,
Try sharing your books, and teaching our creed:
"We first graders work hard, so please don't distract us.
When learning to read, we need plenty of practice!"*

In summary, the exemplary first-grade professionals in our study taught more significant content and used more varied types of instruction each day than typical first-grade teachers (Block, 2001a). Our research additionally found that the ability of these excellent teachers to create well-conceived and well-structured lessons was the most important domain of instructional skill that distinguished them from less effective first-grade teachers.

---

*Used with permission of Nancy Warmbold Zamor and the International Reading Association.

What Students Have to Say about Exemplary Literacy Teachers at the First-Grade Level

"Ms. N let me practice reading every night at home. She let me use a marker to keep my place when I needed it, and helped me break down words. When I used to come to an 'i' and 'e,' I got confused when I tried to sound them out. She taught me why, and now I don't."—Joshua, a first grader in New Mexico

SECOND GRADE

Dominant Lesson-Planning Strategy: INVENTORS

We found outstanding second grade literacy teachers to be *Inventors* who differentiate and plan more creative methods of teaching decoding and comprehension than do their counterparts at other grade levels. They take such actions because they understand that for concepts to be effectively learned at the second-grade level, they must be taught creatively. Many students who have not yet learned basic beginning reading skills by the time they reach the second grade will not do so if their teacher uses lesson formats similar to those employed by exemplary preschool, kindergarten, or even first-grade teachers. Such second-grade teachers understand this fact, so they teach in ways that students would not have experienced in prior years. They are exceptionally talented at creating new strategies to teach basic decoding, vocabulary, comprehension, and fluency skills.

Our research also found that these professionals continually reinforce phonetic principles through oral and written language situations that arise from their use of novel methods and examples with children. For instance, these teachers systematically write new words on the board that they say during lessons. Because of this, the students start to ask the teacher to write and define such words or words they cannot read as soon as the word enters the discussion. This practice also stimulates students ease and frequent desire to ask the teacher other questions about literacy. In these classrooms, many lessons are initiated by student queries about how to read better. These lessons are often innovatively crafted wordplays or word sorts, and employ adaptations of current events games so that students can continue to enjoy learning how to read and write. Our research showed that exemplary second-grade teachers can also be differentiated from their less effective peers by their creative use of journals and writing lessons to teach reading and of writing to teach reading. Journal writing lessons vary almost daily, contain assignments that cannot be completed in one setting, and involve student-generated topics.

When we asked students in these teachers' classes what were the most important parts of their literacy lessons, and the ways in which their teacher taught them that helped them learn the most they reported that

- "Mr. N challenged us to do our best."
- "Ms. T gave us more homework that helped me learn and made sure that we knew how to do it before we left to go home."
- "When we had to do a special unit, she demonstrated how to do it so everybody could understand."
- "When Ms. S returned our homework, she walked us through it."
- "When people were having trouble spacing their letters, she let them space with a Popsicle stick."

- "When we had to do a reading project, she did it first, like doing a full example, so we all could understand it."
- "When Ms. A read a book that was complicated, she explained it as she went."

What Students Have to Say about Exemplary Literacy Teachers at the Second-Grade Level

"He let us read books and the Internet in pairs so I could learn all the words. Thanks to Mr. S I always had someone right beside me to turn to and to say "wow!"—Chad, a second grader in Maryland

THIRD GRADE

Dominant Lesson-Planning Strategy: CATALYSTS

Exemplary third-grade teachers are masters at teaching abstract concepts by making them more concrete through reteaching them in different-sized groups and using peers' voices to explain them at times. Unlike with exemplary first-grade teachers, however, these peer explanations are more frequently given as rephrased examples during small group and whole class instructional settings. Students also make charts of literacy processes that are placed around the room so less able readers can read about how to perform literacy process. These are in student vernacular and supplement the rich descriptions and think alouds of the exemplary teacher. These professionals are *Catalysts*, distinguished by their superior abilities to state expectations clearly and to obtain highly effective levels of student participation even when the teacher is not present with a literacy group.

Outstanding teachers at this grade level also have the ability to stimulate deeper thinking about the text by asking students to defend their positions. They develop critical thinking skills among their students, enabling them to learn how to read textbooks independently with a high degree of comprehension. We found their use of "think-alouds" to be one of the highly effective methods they implement to attain these goals. Examples of the kinds of think-alouds that add to the quality of their lessons appreciably appear in Figure 10.1.

Exemplary third-grade teachers also are masterful at planning lessons that encourage students to take risks. They use their own passion for learning as a model to help students challenge themselves. By describing how they are thinking creatively and critically as they read, as well as experiences from their own lives involving literacy, became critical thinkers, exemplary third-grade teachers create within students a quest for comprehending subjects as thoroughly as possible. They display exceptional talent in moving students from dependent to independent learning as well as in simultaneously making abstract concepts more concrete. They do so by often modulating in several distinct ways thinking processes-in-action, as they read. They would then ask students to try to comprehend or decode using the same processes. They also elicit quality participation from their pupils at the onset of activities by explaining ably and clearly the expectations that they have established for each student or group.

For those students who experience difficulty in decoding, these teachers develop single lessons that begin with one-syllable, and then progress to three-syllable words and depend on synthetic or analytical phonics instructional methods until individual children discover that reading largely consists in fitting together a lot of different decoding, comprehension, vocabulary, and fluency thinking processes in union.

What Students Have to Say about Exemplary Literacy Teachers at the Thurd-Grade Level

"Mr. Thurman makes sure that we have all our skills down. He lets us write stories that we thought of. He asks us to explain how we learned to read something until we really understand how to think like that all the time we're readin'."—Samantha, a third-grader in Georgia

FIGURE 10.1. Building More Effective Lessons Skill Development Chart: Creating Effective "Think-Alouds"

The focus of this activity is to build both comprehension and oral expression. Students need to develop the kinds of strategies that good readers use to extract meaning from material. By "thinking aloud" teachers can model the productive strategies that they use to understand important texts, and thus can encourage students to develop the same self-monitoring strategies as they comprehend.

1. To begin this classroom activity, watch a videotaped television, award-winning drama plot. Periodically stop the video, using the pause button after a particular scene. Then perform a "think-aloud" about how you are inferring, summarizing, and connecting details to gain deep meaning from the program to students. There are many possible strategies to perform exemplary think-alouds.

   - DEMONSTRATE HOW TO USE PRIOR KNOWLEDGE.
     For example, "Now I know the robber will get caught because it's a mystery, and this is always the ending of the mystery genre.

   - SHOW HOW TO MONITOR COMPREHENSION STRATEGIES.
     For example, "I'm not sure I really understood the part about carbohydrates and energy. Maybe I should wait to form an opinion about it, until I get more information."

   - DESCRIBE HOW TO USE CONTEXT CLUES TO GUESS AT UNFAMILIAR VOCABULARY.
     For example, "I really don't know what 'fatigued' means, but from the way it's used in the sentences spoken by the main character, Leo, I would guess it means 'tired.' "

   - DEMONSTRATE HOW TO PREDICT WHAT MAY HAPPEN NEXT, EVEN IF IT TURNS OUT NOT TO BE CORRECT.
     For example, "From what I've seen so far, I think the man in the blue shirt is going to win the prize. The several clues that make me think so were . . . "
     Exemplary teachers used these think-aloud techniques on a regular basis, modeling one or two reading strategies per lesson.

2. Following this demonstration, encourage students to try these same thinking processes to monitor their comprehension by asking them to read the last chapter from the book upon which the televised version was based. As they read, walk around the room and ask each individual to perform a think-aloud about the thinking processes they are using to comprehend. When all have finished reading, show the conclusion to the TV version. Have student defend which ending was better. Next, using a different highly predictable program or book from the same genre (they'll have more success with this type of show, especially in the beginning), stop the tape after several brief episodes. Ask students:

   - What do you think will happen next?

   - Why do you think so? What is your proof?

   - Do you have any questions?

   Conclude this lesson by reinforcing your literacy objective (e.g., students will enjoy predicting future events in a more free-flowing way. Tell them that they are using very complex comprehension skills and succeeding in monitoring these processes as they read and view.

Adapted from National Captioning Institute (1990). Copyright 1990 by National Captioning Institute. Adapted by permission.

FOURTH GRADE

Dominant Lesson-Planning Strategy: OPTION QUARTERBACKS

In football, *Option Quarterbacks* can either hand the ball to a runner or pass it to a receiver. In the classrooms that we observed, exemplary fourth-grade literacy teachers were found to be masterful at creating lessons that establish many goals and strategies for each literacy activity, from which students can choose their own goals. In this way these teachers' lessons create several "options" from which they and their students can select to build the students' ability to assume responsibility to learn more about literacy as well as to learn from reading alone. In the process, these professionals continue to teach students to be independent learners when working on long-term projects. An example of a self-assessment form that was used by one of the outstanding teachers in our study to reach this goal appears in Figure 10.2.

Our research found that such teachers introduce and reteach a variety of strategies in the same lesson. Unlike exemplary first-grade teachers who also include several literacy strategies in a single lesson, exemplary fourth-grade teachers teach the majority of these strategies at the start of a lesson, rather than waiting for student to ask about what to do at specific difficult points in a text, which is when first-grade teachers would be more likely to do so. Both groups of exemplary teachers implement lessons targeted to meet students' exact needs. The difference is that expert first-grade teachers are masterful at meeting these needs at the time they emerge; fourth-grade exemplary professionals spend many hours in creating data in need assessments prior to planning their highly effective lessons. These teachers also focus their lessons on larger, more encompassing objectives than peers at lower grade levels. Sample themes are how to become better citizens and help others in the world. As one of the exemplary fourth-grade teachers in our study affirmed: "The students have to know that this is their classroom—and their lives. It isn't just integrating reading and writing that makes our studies authentic or even reading about topics that are important to my students individually or collectively. What connects us as a community of learners who respect and support each other's strengths and weaknesses is that we view the classroom as a place where we all work and grow. We work on projects that we own, and that is very important to us."

What Students Have to Say about Exemplary Literacy Teachers at the Fourth-Grade Level

"Ms. Dodge let us have as much homework as we wanted, and we could choose what we wanted to do from the list that she gave us."—Carlos, a fourth grader in Texas

FIGURE 10.2. Building More Effective Lessons Skill Development Chart: Self-Assessment Forms for Establishing Differentiated Student Literacy Goals

Dear Students,

Use this self-assessment form when you finish learning a new literacy strategy, or complete the self-assessment by the end of the full week's work. We can then use it to plan next week's instruction.

Student's name: _____ Date: _____

Describe your specific goal for today/this week/this project (circle one) _____

_____

What would you like me to teach you? _____

_____

What do you want to do after you finish reading about [the assignment] as a postreading activity? _____

_____

Complete the following self-assessment:

I met or did not meet my goal because _____

_____

From this experience, I learned _____

_____

My level of satisfaction with what I accomplished today/this week (circle one) in this project is _____

_____

The strategy that worked best for me when I read today was _____

_____ because _____

_____

What I want to learn next is _____

_____

FIFTH GRADE

Dominant Lesson-Planning Strategy: **EMPOWERISTS**

Exemplary fifth-grade literacy teachers are termed *Empowerists*. They are masters at building lessons that instill in students a desire to produce work that is excellent. They regularly teach students how to organize their thoughts, explore, and learn on their own by asking questions of students that require them to think on their feet, on their own, and at high levels of abstraction. The specific questions that they were observed to use to reach these goals appear in Figure 10.3 and can be used in your lessons to increase your students' high-level comprehension abilities. Many teachers who were developing these skills practiced one question from Figure 10.3 each week in a school year until they had mastered the ability to use different questions each week.

These educators also teach students how to organize their thoughts, to explore and learn on their own. Unlike exemplary kindergarten teachers, exemplary fifth-grade teachers do not guide students to these discoveries. Instead they continuously pose challenges through expertly timed questions so students initiate their own desires to discover how to become better readers and more knowledgeable about interesting topics. These teachers also pose thought-provoking questions nonjudgmentally, so that students at all levels of ability can participate. An important ingredient in their literacy lessons is the way in which students are taught how to ask for guidance and how to set and expand the boundaries within which they can best achieve higher levels of literacy through self-governance. The teacher's goal is to guide and shape students' thinking and comprehension strategies in reading and through reading. Teachers empower students to take chances; they hold debates in class, allow students freedom and choice, and meet students' individual needs easily and effectively. Their lessons demonstrate the exceptional skill that fifth-grade teachers must posses as they mix structure with student freedom on a daily basis. They accomplish this objective by empowering pupils to do something important through the use of their higher-level comprehension of materials read. For example, they routinely make students prove their points, to peers, to the principal at their school, and to others. They also have a strong commitment to advance knowledge and people's multifaceted capabilities through the work that they ask students to do.

When we asked fifth-grade students what they appreciated about teachers that were judged to be exemplary, they confirmed these findings. For example, most fifth graders reported that their teachers planned lessons that enabled them to do something worthwhile with what they learned. As a result of their teachers' instruction, the majority of students reported that they imaged pictures in their minds and were thinking to themselves about what they read while they were reading. Most pupils said that their teachers' lessons helped them learn more because they contained better and more concise explanations than did the lessons of teachers who provided instruction to their friends. They also reported that they were able to ask more questions in class about what they had read—questions about what they comprehended and what they didn't.

FIGURE 10.3. Building More Effective Lessons
Skill Development Chart: Reflecting Questions Back to Students
to Increase Their Higher-Level Comprehension Abilities

Elaboration

Does this make you think of anything else you read? Why?

Would you like to be one of the people in this event? Who? Why?

Did you like this more or less than the last thing you read? Why?

What parts of this have you especially liked or disliked?

What did you mean by _____? Can you give me an example?

If _____ happened, what else could happen?

Does this story remind you of any other one? Why? What specific characteristics do they have in common?

Did the author make you feel any specific emotion?

Can you describe the _____?

How could you advertise this book?

If you had a chance to talk to this author, what would you speak to him or her about?

Why do you suppose the author gave this title? Can you think of another appropriate title?

Why is this an important story to share?

Metacognition (thinking about thinking)

How would you feel if _____ happened?

What were your thoughts when you decided whether to _____ or _____? How did you decide?

Why did you choose this selection to read?

Do you think this story could really happen? Explain.

After reading this story, has your perception or view of _____ changed? Explain.

Can you describe your thinking? I need to hear more details.

What makes you think he or she _____? How do you know this?

What do you know that you did not know before reading this?

Did your thoughts and feelings change as you were reading? How and why?

How did you apply what you already knew as you read?

Problem solving

What do you need to do next to become a better reader?

Can you think of another way we could do this?

How did you solve this decoding, vocabulary, comprehension, or fluency problem?

(cont.)

FIGURE 10.3. *(cont.)*

What did you do when you came to these difficult words?
What did you do when you got stuck?
What did you do when you did not understand the content or context?
How did you come up with this, and what helped you the most?
How could we go about finding out if this is true?

Supporting answers

Why is this solution better than that one?
Yes, that's right—but how did you know?
What are your reasons for saying that?
What do you (or author) mean by _____?
Why does this go here instead of there?
Do you have good evidence for believing that?
How did you know that?

Exemplary fifth-grade teachers were also found to let their students write in different genres more frequently than did less able teachers at this grade levels. These writings increased student comprehension, both on achievement tests as well as in the judgment of the students whom they taught. They also created lessons designed to build in students a desire to read more. Their objective is being realized, as our study found, and this goal is occurring for their students at a significantly higher level than for students in the same schools who had less effective teachers.

What Students Have to Say about Exemplary Literacy Teachers at the Fifth-Grade Level

"What we did in Mr. Escamilla's classroom was fun. We got to do something with what we understood from the books and about what we thought after we read the books. This made me know I can be smart when I read."—LeMarcus, a fifth grader in New York

CHAPTER ELEVEN

THE CHOICE

Early in her career, Cathy, one of the coauthors of this book, was confronted with a problem. When she tried to read research studies, she did not understand significant portions of them. At that time, this lack of comprehension was due to her limited knowledge of research and statistical procedures.

Cathy had two choices. She could do nothing to address this shortcoming. She could easily justify such a decision. After all, at that period in her life, she had already enjoyed a great deal of success both as an elementary school teacher and as a university teacher. She was also quite busy and had little time to add anything new to her already very full plate. And, besides, she could go to colleagues who knew those subjects when there was something that she didn't understand.

Alternatively, she could take actions to address this shortcoming. She could begin a process to improve her knowledge base relating to research. As a consequence of this change, she would then not only be able to comprehend the nuances of research but also be able to properly conduct research investigations herself. And, as for the time needed to acquire this skill, Cathy could lessen her involvement in some things and she could work a bit longer each week while this process was occurring.

Cathy carefully thought about the pros and cons of each of these options. Then, she reached a decision: she would expend the time and effort required to become knowledgeable about, and adept in, research.

Cathy's decision has proved to be a wise one. After it was made, as Paul Harvey would say, "The rest was history." At the time of this writing, Cathy is the author or coauthor of 28 research-based literacy books and 93 professional evidence-based, peer reviewed articles, chapters, or curriculum projects. Research is the keystone of these works. Had it not been for the decision that Cathy made to make this change, it is doubtful that today she would be a Professor of Education at Texas Christian University and a member of the Board of Directors of the International Reading Association.

We have told this story because, in many respects, you are now in a position akin to the one Cathy was in. Just as she was at the time when she made her decision, we are sure that your career as a teacher has been replete with positive achievements. The question confronting you is: Are you satisfied with your present level of success or do you wish to take those efforts "to the next level" of success?

If you desire to make no significant changes in your teaching behaviors, then you do not need to read any further in this book. If you are uncertain, or have decided to become a more effective teacher of literacy, please continue reading this chapter.

Based upon the actions that you have already completed by implementing ideas in earlier chapters of this book, you have both ample and accurate information to respond to the question, Who am I being as a teacher? We have also supplied you with information about the characteristics of exemplary teachers who provide literacy instruction at the same grade level as you currently do.

You would be well served to keep several things in mind as you review and think about these data. The initial question that faces you is whether or not you wish to continue to offer literacy instruction at the grade level where you are presently teaching. As you mull this question over in your mind, you should look at what the NELTA data in Chapter 4 revealed about you. For example, did it indicate your *present* traits would be more suitable to a position as a literacy teacher at another grade level? Or, did it reveal that the grade at which you presently teach is the one most appropriate to your professional qualities? Let's examine both of these questions a bit.

If the NELTA conveyed that you and your present literacy teaching assignment are a good "match," we both *commend* and *challenge* you. We *commend* you for using your talents with students at a grade level that is appropriate for your literacy teaching strengths. We *challenge* you to use this congruity between you and your teaching assignment as a springboard to enjoy even greater success as a literacy provider. This action can come in the form of professional development. We urge you to ask yourself: What literacy knowledge needs or instructional implementation shortcomings do I have that are limiting my effectiveness as a teacher? While such an analysis can be difficult for some individuals, we are convinced that, after you work toward the professional needs that you have identified, both you and your students will be glad that you had the courage to begin this process.

For those persons to whom the NELTA indicated that your *present traits* are more consistent with those exhibited by exemplary teachers at a grade level different from your present one, you have three choices.

First, you can elect to remain in your present assignment and initiate a plan to change. With the benchmarks presented in Chapters 5–10, you have clear targets for improvement. By examining where your behavior levels are in each of these domains, you can compare how you "measure up" to the exemplary counterparts whose profiles were presented in earlier chapters. Priorities can be established as to the order in which you plan to eliminate or reduce behaviors that are less effective for the grade level at which you teach. Additionally, you can identify the behaviors that you plan to enhance so that they will become a more important facet of your literacy teaching style.

A second alternative is also available to you. When analyzing your present pedagogical behaviors, you can make a determination as to which grade level they are most appropriate for literacy instruction. After this assessment has occurred, you can begin to examine whether this grade level is one that you might like to teach in the future.

We recommend that the aforementioned process not be quickly conducted. It has been our experience that overhasty decisions often produce less-than-ideal outcomes.

Rather, we suggest that several different but related actions be taken over a period of time as this important decision is being reached. What types of actions can be taken?

Colleagues have found it helpful to begin this process by examining the literacy curriculum for which you would be instructionally accountable if you opted to teach at this "new" grade level. Then, you may wish to *carefully* review the materials customarily used to teach literacy at that grade level. You will note the word "carefully" in the preceding sentence. Cursory scans will usually lead to superficial conclusions being reached. Instead, look at these materials with a question in mind—namely, Would I find it professionally satisfying to teach these literacy strategies to students?

Other actions that could be subsequently taken and that may prove helpful include observing skillful teachers providing literacy instruction at that grade; conversing with such teachers as to the joys and challenges that they experience in providing literacy instruction at this grade; and teaching a literacy lesson to the students at this "new" grade level.

A third course is also available. You can choose neither to alter your current set of behaviors nor to move to a different grade level to teach literacy. Clearly, this nonaction is, in our judgment, an unacceptable option. We believe that neither your students nor your satisfaction as a professional would be positively served by it.

As stated in Chapter 4, Tolstoy said, "Everyone dreams of changing humanity but no one dreams of changing himself." You have spent a considerable amount of time and expended your energy on reading a book that has focused upon precisely that—change. We hope that you are convinced that this book's content is based upon sound, important, and conclusive research. The potential benefits that you can derive from this content are enormous. You have an opportunity to become appreciably more effective as a literacy teacher. You also have a chance to be remembered by your students as *the teacher* who gave the gift of literacy to them.

In Chapter 2, we recounted our fond memories of two of our teachers, Mrs. McLaughlin and Sister Gertrude, who each had a monumental impact on our respective lives. Do you want to have a comparable legacy for the students that you will teach in the future?

We hope you will answer this question with a firm and convincing "Yes. I do!" If you did, we congratulate you for this response. We wish you well in pursuing a major step toward attaining your next level of success as a literacy teacher.

We wish you well in this important journey!

RATIONALE FOR THIS STUDY

Thus far in this book we have discussed exemplary teachers at every level from preschool through grade 5. We have also examined your teaching proficiencies. We did this because we wanted you to become more knowledgeable about your colleagues in the 21st century, across the country, who are attaining great results in giving the gift of literacy to children. Although we presented this information in the six major domains constituting exemplary literacy instruction, we did not want you to think each description and chapter was an island unto itself. All of them together represent a composite that has been based on two intensive research studies that were conducted over a 2-year period.

THE RESEARCH OF THIS BOOK: HOW THE FIRST STUDY WAS CONDUCTED

The purpose of this study was to create a descriptive database of preschool to grade 5 teaching expertise. It was based on instructional qualities that distinguished highly effective from less effective literacy teachers employed in the same schools and socioeconomic neighborhoods. Because students profit from particular types of instruction at specific stages in their literacy development (Anders, Hoffman, & Duffy, 2000; Snow, Burns, & Griffin, 1998), it is reasonable to assume that particular talents are required of teachers who serve students at different stages along the literacy developmental continuum.

It has been determined that several abilities distinguish highly effective first-grade teachers from their less effective peers (Block, 2001a, 2001b, 2001c, 2001d; Pressley, Allington, Wharton-McDonald, Block, & Morrow, 2001). Students of more competent teachers scored significantly higher on end-of-grade-1 and end-of-grade-2 literacy assessments than schoolmates whose teachers did not possess as many traits of expertise (Block, 2001a, 2001b). Data in this study were based on 90-minute observations. It was found that highly effective teachers implemented an additional strategy involving students in learning, on average, once every 8 minutes that was not executed by less effective peers. These teachers did not rely on curriculum alone, nor did they employ a single broad-brush approach for all students (Block, 2001a; Duffy & Hoffman, 1999; Juel & Minden-Cupp, 2000; Pressley et al., 2001). How they, as well as teachers from preschool through grade 5, initiate such systematic, thoughtful expertise had not been fully analyzed prior to the study reported in this book, this Appendix, and reported in Block, Oakar, and Hurt (2002).

During the past 5 years, the need to create indices of teaching expertise has increased radically, for several reasons. First, more educators in the United States than ever before are being evaluated for merit pay increases through peer observations of their teaching effectiveness. In California the first statewide peer-review program was enacted on March 30, 1998, and Ohio followed with initiative in 1999 (Archer & Blair, 2001). As a result, educators and legislators requested "empirical data upon which highly effective practices at individual grade levels could be assessed" (California Congressional Record, 1998, p. 13). "Few studies tease out how teachers teach ... and why something is working" (Expert Panel Testimonies Transcript, 1998, p. 39). These data are important because legislators and policymakers must better come to terms with the indicators of teaching literacy expertise.

Research has demonstrated that teaching expertise makes a significant difference in the rate and depth of students' literacy growth and that highly effective educators share similar characteristics (Block, 2001a; Bond & Dykstra, 1997[1967]; International Reading Association, 2000; Pressley et al., 2001; Ruddell, 1997). The National Reading Panel (1999) and IRA (2000) recommended that "educators seek out teachers who best exemplify solid teaching, support their work, and consider their successes" (NRP, 1999, p. 20).

The National Commission on Teaching and America's Future (1998) described a second need. This panel stated that the education profession must "reach across the barriers that separate practitioners, policymakers, and the public, and seek more comprehensive, transformational changes regarding teachers' craft, its structures, and possibilities for teaching and learning" (pp. 5–6). There is a demand to prepare

> a new kind of teacher—one who must think harder, longer, deeper—in order to instruct diverse learners in responsive and responsible ways. Even when teachers [know] what to change, [such change] depends, as Au and Carroll observed (1997), on getting beyond generalities to specifics. . . . Much is said about what students should know and need to learn in relation to standards, which few literacy educators would dispute (e.g., flexibility in applying different reading strategies), but there is scant information about what teachers actually [do] to develop flexibility among a roomful of diverse learners [from grades preschool through grade 5]. (Roskos, Risko, & Vukelich, 1998, pp. 233–234)

How do highly effective literacy teachers unite their training, professional knowledge about students' needs and interests, as well as the social dynamics of classroom interactions to create quality instruction? We need to learn more about how theory (the "shoulds" and "visions") is embedded effectively in the "have to"'s and "is"'s of practice. While setting standards for content and performance is an important first step, we must study the processes of expertise in action (Biddle, 1997). To understand teaching, we must analyze what the best of the best literacy practitioners are doing in their classrooms to increase literacy achievement (Ayers, 1996). The teaching career, like the medical vocation, began with one educator and one physician, respectively, addressing all educational and medical requests in a community. Today's teachers need more information and research-based expertise to select more wisely among, and excel within, the multitude of specializations in the profession (Block, 2001d; Block & Mangieri, 1996; Costa, 2001).

A third need emanates from a recurring educational issue and may be the most important rationale for this study. In many countries, students are required to attain a higher level of literacy by age 10 than in the past. Many who do not achieve at this standard are held back a grade (Atkin & Black, 1997). If we can identify grade-level indices of teaching expertise and implement these findings, it stands to reason that more children would receive consistently effective instruction at every grade level. Such data could also provide preservice elementary education majors with information to make more informed decisions about the grade levels they want to teach. As a result, educators' most valued and advanced skills and talents could be used more strategically. Veteran teachers might be able to remain in the profession longer, and beginning teachers might have greater opportunity to accrue more of the experience necessary for high levels of performance (Berliner, 2001). Instead of leaving teaching, many could elect to transfer either up or down grade levels where their teaching expertise would be called upon continuously.

To learn more about how highly effective teachers, from preschool to grade 5, organize classrooms that maximize students' literacy skills, we sought research that answered these questions:

1. Do indicators of expertise in teaching literacy differ by the grade level being taught?
2. Do practitioners and researchers agree upon indicators of teaching expertise that lead to the greatest gains in students' literacy skills from preschool through grade 5?

3. Can more specific information about teaching expertise be obtained so that educators can make more informed decisions about (1) which grade level most consistently utilizes their talents and skills best and (2) how to advance their expertise in very specific ways?

Theoretical Background

This study was based on two bodies of knowledge. The first was data concerning the qualities that define effective teaching; the second was an analysis of studies that discerned indicators of expert behavior. For more than a hundred years, highly effective teachers have helped students enter the world of literacy with ease and high levels of success (Smith, 1989). During the 1960s researchers examined programs, curricula, and philosophical approaches to discern whether specific instructional materials produced significant gains in literacy achievement (Bond & Dykstra, 1997[1967]). It was concluded that the type of materials used in the classroom was not the key differentiator. While certain curricular features enhanced students' literacy success, distinct reading curricula and approaches produced both good and bad results, depending upon how well a teacher implemented them. Teaching abilities—far more than the types of materials used—were found to be the major contributors to students' literacy success.

Recent studies reaffirmed that to improve reading instruction we must examine teaching expertise rather than expect a panacea in the form of materials (e.g., Allington, Guice, Michelson, Baker, & Li, 1996; Baumann, Hoffman, Moon, & Duffy-Hester, 1998; Block, Joyner, Joy, & Gaines, 2002; Block & Mangieri, 1996; Hoffman et al., 1998; Sacks & Mergendoller, 1997). These studies also demonstrated that typical primary grade teachers during the 1990s used multiple approaches. They embraced literature-based perspectives; combined quality children's literature, nonfictional trade books, and basal anthologies as their curricula; taught phonics in the context of children's literature; and "practiced a philosophy of disciplined eclecticism" (Baumann et al., 1998, p. 647).

In the new century, educators are seeking to develop teacher instructional expertise in literacy that is even more advanced and specialized (Archer & Blair, 2001). For instance, at the Texas Education Agency (State Department of Education), as in other domestic and international educational institutions, the traditional elementary teaching certificate (a kindergarten through grade 8 licensure) has been discontinued. It was replaced with five demarcated certifications at the elementary level and a separate middle school certificate (to teach students aged 13–16). A future elementary education major may elect to become (1) a specialist in early childhood literacy (licensed to teach students aged 2 to 9), (2) a specialist in intermediate elementary childhood (certified to teach from ages 10 through 14), or (3) a specialist in one of three categories of special needs that elementary students face. In the future, students seeking the bachelor of elementary education degree will no longer be expected to master the broad band of knowledge and methodologies required to teach literacy to students who range in age from 2 to 16.

Researchers have also examined teachers' philosophical values and theoretical orientations in an attempt to identify teaching expertise (Block 2001a, 2001c; Sacks & Mergendoller, 1997). Does believing in one philosophical approach over another produce superior literacy gains for students? Data indicated that such was not the case. Even when kindergarten and first-grade teachers espoused diametrically opposed philosophies, they (1) spent about the same amount of time engaged in whole-group and small-group lessons; (2) taught the same content using similar activities; and (3) employed comparable teaching methodologies (e.g., direct teaching, shared reading, computer-assisted instruction, process writing lessons, and worksheets). Moreover, teachers who adhered to a direct teaching approach had approximately the same ratio of teacher talk to student talk as well as rate of student engagement as educators who advocated a literature-based philosophy (Block, 2001a; Sacks & Mergendoller, 1997).

If curriculum approaches and philosophical orientations do not determine the relative success of literacy teachers, perhaps individual indices of teaching expertise can. Recent analyses of instructional traits suggest that highly effective teaching demands a complex repertoire of expertise (Block, 2001c; Pressley et al., 2001).

Highly successful teachers, regardless of the grade level at which they teach, possess common characteristics (for reviews, see National Board of Professional Teaching Standards, 1997; Ruddell, 1997). They (1) take risks (Wilson & Ball, 1997); (2) are energetic (Faust & Kieffer, 1998); (3) teach with flexibility and understanding, to meet individual students' needs (Ruddell, 1997); (4) are passionate about the subject(s) they teach (Bruner, 1986); (5) are committed to, care about, and advocate for actions that improve their students' lives (Lee, 2001; Pressley et al., 2001); (6) develop highly effective instructional repertoires (Porter & Brophy, 1988); (7) scaffold frequently (Berliner & Tikunoff, 1996; Block & Mangieri, 1996; Medley, 1977); (8) support pupils in their first attempts to learn new concepts (Block & Mangieri, 1996; Cazden, 1994; Porter & Brophy, 1988); (9) maintain high expectations of themselves and their students (Block & Mangieri, 1996; Erickson & Smith, 1991; Lee, 2001; Leibert, 1991; Ruddell, 1997); (10) provide clear purposes and directions (Block & Mangieri, 1996; Good & Grouws, 1975; Porter & Brophy, 1988; Rosenshine & Furst, 1971; Ruddell, 1997); (11) understand child and adolescent development; (12) believe that all can achieve literacy (International Reading Association, 2000; Lee, 2001); (13) assess children and relate progress to previous experiences (International Reading Association, 2000); and (14) know how and when to combine methods that result in accelerated literacy growth (International Reading Association, 2000).

Recent research also suggested that pedagogical knowledge was contextualized by grade level more than by materials used. For example, Block (2000c) identified 12 teaching traits that distinguished first-grade teachers who helped students sustain their statistically significant literacy gains until the end of second grade, regardless of materials used in either of these grades' classrooms. Similarly, exemplary performances at the eighth-grade level would not automatically transfer if that teacher were assigned to fourth grade (Berliner, 1994). Allington, Block, and Morrow (2000) also found that the effectiveness of fourth-grade teachers was not dependent upon whether or not they chose to work in departmental or self-contained settings.

Work to understand how such teaching expertise develops began more than 100 years ago (Harter, 1899). Numerous propositions have been offered since that time, and we have learned the following (Berliner, 1994; Chi, Glaser, & Farr, 1988; Glaser, 1987, 1990). Exemplary teachers (1) possess knowledge that was developed over thousands of hours of experiential learning (which apparently requires more than 3 years to accrue, with 10-year veterans typically amassing some 10,000 hours of classroom experience [Berliner, 1994]); (2) structure problems through qualitatively different and richer patterns than less expert educators (Polya, 1954); (3) highlight the meaningful components in a learning process (Block, 2001c); (4) are skilled opportunistic planners who change approaches rapidly when appropriate (Pressley et al., 2001); (5) can rapidly impose meaning on ambiguous situations (Chi, Glaser, & Farr, 1988); and (6) engage automatic behaviors and self-regulatory processes that enhance student learning (Berliner, 1994).

Scientists proposed that exemplary performance develops in stages (see Dreyfus & Dreyfus [1986] and Shuell [1990] for a review of these theories).

Novices and beginning teachers (stage 1 in Berliner's [1994] theory concerning the development of exemplary performances) implement global educational rules that they were taught in a broad-based blanket manner, such as always allowing 6 seconds of wait time for a student to respond and identifying students' interests with a survey on the first day of school. Novice teachers structure classrooms to conform to the rules that they were taught (Berliner, 2001; Mangieri & Block, 1994).

Advanced beginners (stage 2), who likely emerge during the second and third year in the profession, develop strategic knowledge. They know when to depart from, and when to adhere to, the global rules that they were taught. However, it was found that second- and third-year teachers often have not yet developed the sense of what is important (Benner, 1986). (For more in-depth information, see the case study that Bullough [1989] presented of one teacher's transition from novice to advanced beginner.)

A few third-year and many fourth-year teachers reach a level of expertise labeled *competency* (stage 3). Researchers generally agree that competent teachers can be discerned in that they consistently (1) set priorities, (2) choose sensible methods for reaching goals, and, (3) determine what is relevant to their immediate context from research, philosophies, and methodologies (Bents & Bents, 1990; Glaser, 1987). Novices and advanced beginners share more traits in common than do advanced beginners and competent teachers because the former have not developed these three traits or a sense of professional confidence (see Humphrey, 2003, for an in-depth description of one teacher's transition from novice to competent stages of teaching proficiencies). For the ability to willfully choose what to do and to take full responsibility for their decisions, advanced beginners demonstrated a need for more experiential successes (Berliner, 2001). For these reasons, it seems reasonable to assume that teachers must have at least 3 years of experience before reliable indicators of exemplary teaching can be identified.

At stage 4, *proficiency*, intuition develops. Proficient teachers recognize numerous similarities among events that teachers with less proficiency do not perceive (Berliner, 1994; Block, 2001a; Pressley et al., 2001). It is only at the *expert level* (stage 5), however, that a state of fluid, flawless teaching develops. Experts alone "seem to know where to be and what to do at the right time" (Berliner, 1994, p. 167). They become one with their content and students without having to consciously choose what to attend to and do. Such abilities are obtained from "knowledge in action" (first described in the theory of Schon [1983, p. 19]) and tacit wisdom in problem solving (Polya, 1954). Excellent teachers learn from experience "what works . . . and what does not work and they use only what works" (Pressley et al., 2001, p. 11). As compared with those at lower levels of competence, experts more thoroughly understand the context in which they teach, and plan more activities in a single day (Berliner et al., 1988). They also develop automaticity for repetitive operations (Glaser, 1987, 1990; Leinhardt & Greeno, 1986; Pressley et al., 2001). For instance, they review concepts in one-third less time than novices (Knapp, 1995; Krabbe & Tullgren, 1989).

Expert educators implement more instructional strategies based on social and individual student cues than do novices. The specific differences that exist, and distinct clues that experts use, at different grade levels, had not been documented prior to this study (Berliner, 1994; Glaser, 1987; Housner & Griffey, 1985).

Borko and Livingston (1988) also found that expert teachers' improvisational performances depended upon quickly generated examples that connected students' comments with the lesson's objective, and they maintained closer proximity to students (Berliner, 1994; Hawkins & Sharpe, 1995; Nelson, 1988). The strategies that they used in different literacy activities, for students of different ages, have not been documented (Block, 2001a; Pressley et al., 2001). Past studies have demonstrated that a vast amount of experiential learning is necessary but not necessarily sufficient to develop such expertise. How do literacy teachers in preschool and fifth-grade classrooms relate to students and generate effective examples? How do they improvise, reteach, motivate, sustain lessons, relate to students, and create classroom climates based on students' cognitive, affective, and social clues? The answers to these questions could shed light on the complex nature of teaching expertise.

Several issues must be addressed before grade-sensitive indicators can be identified. The first is how to identify expert literacy teachers. In the past some researchers have asked teachers to assess their own competencies (e.g., Dillman, 1978; Warwick & Lininger, 1975). Such self-evaluations have been demonstrated to contain biases, ingratiation, deception, self-degradation, self-ascension, and a tendency to respond in ways that conformed to dominant cultural mores in a school, district, and nation. Other researchers turned to student performance as the barometer to discern teaching effectiveness, without controlling for numerous external influences that affect literacy achievement. For instance, socioeconomic environments alter literacy growth, not only because of the large disparity existing in the available resources but also because affluent students tend to perform better on standardized tests even when teaching expertise is largely lacking in the instruction that they receive (e.g., Biddle, 1997; Block, 2001a; Wilkinson, 1998; Wolcott, 1988).

To illustrate, by 1992 the disparity in financial support among U.S. schools where students averaged in the 95th as compared to the 5th percentile on standardized reading tests, was statistically significant. The contrast in funding was startling: students who lived in rich communities characterizes by generous funding initiatives attended public schools that spent $15,000 or more per student per year, while pupils residing in poorer communities in less affluent states had to learn comparable material despite having financial resources of only $3,000 or less per student per year. Highly effective teaching in the latter settings appeared to be crucial to student success (Biddle, 1997). To differentiate these and other potential factors, it is important to identify multiple indicators of teaching expertise in school districts around the world that represent English-speaking communities and that serve a wide variety of student ability levels with highly variable resources available.

The second issue is that studies must focus attention on the centrality of the teacher (as opposed to the centrality of a particular set of instructional materials, approaches, or philosophical orientations). The transformation of expert literacy instruction "demands teachers who understand the complexity of teaching, who respect students they teach, and who believe in the endless possibility of transformation for high academic achievement for all students" (Lee, 2001, pp. 13–14). This theoretical orientation does not diminish the active role that students must necessarily play in constructing their own literacy (Moll, 1990; Vygotsky, 1962, 1967; Wertsch, 1991). Nonetheless, our study is based on the proposition that what students achieve in literacy depends greatly on the instruction that they receive, the classroom context created, and the actions taken by their teachers. Teachers' expertise goes far in determining the quality of students' instructional episodes (Lee, 2001).

Lastly, the identification of teaching expertise must be based on the assumption that effective literacy teachers "have a privileged understanding of literacy instruction in part because their teaching is based on many decisions about what works in classrooms" (Pressley, Rankin, & Yokoi, 1996, p. 365). To date, we know that it takes at least 3 years for this privileged understanding to develop (Berliner, 1994). Although expert teachers know what they do to advance their students' literacy—continuously seek to improve, adapt instruction more frequently than less effective peers, correct teaching errors, maintain high standards for student self-management and time on task (Block, 2001a), and situate their actions in effective learning environments (Brown, Collins, & Duguid, 1989)—we must identify how these actions are accomplished within the predisposed developmental needs of students at each stage along the literacy continuum.

Method: Procedures and Data Analyses

The current study was a macroanalysis of reading instruction in 647 localities, preschool through grade 5. We followed the principles and procedures of expert performance studies (e.g., Berliner, 1994; Block, 2001b; deGroot, 1966; Pressley et al., 1996; Pressley et al., 2001; Rankin-Erickson & Pressley, 2000). The procedures were enhanced beyond prior studies to include four phases of Delphi analysis. We also took to heart the recommendations of Flippo (2001) that new policies will be enhanced if they are informed by both research and practice, and therefore both practitioners and researchers were included in our data collection.

Phase 1: Compiling a Master List of Indicators of Teaching Expertise

In Phase 1 we obtained a detailed description of effective literacy instruction by soliciting the instructional practices of highly effective literacy teachers in seven English-speaking countries through a Delphi point-by-point analysis. The Delphi technique is a statistical method for structuring a group communication process so that a group of individuals as a whole can describe complex phenomena by providing professional judgment and feedback to the development of agreed-upon practices with complete anonymity. We asked supervisors of literacy instruction in public schools to analyze episodes of instruction that they had observed to identify teaching traits that distinguished the best educators at a specific grade. We selected a geographically diverse sample to avoid bias and to gain generalizability.

To identify teaching literacy expertise, we contacted the International Reading Association for a list of its members who (1) possessed a doctoral or master's degree with a specialization in elementary literacy and (2) had served as a supervisor of literacy instruction in a school district in an English-speaking country for at least 4 years. To be selected, school district literacy supervisors also had to indicate that they had attended symposia, sessions, and preconvention institutes of the 1998 and 1999 annual meetings of the International Reading Association. This attendance was an indicator that they were making a commitment to stay current with the latest research-based practices. In addition, every supervisor had to have completed at least 36 hours of advanced training in literacy research and pedagogy.

We were given 793 names, and 647 of these people completed all segments of the study. The members of the sample who were eliminated were not significantly statistically different from the research group in terms of the number of years of teaching experience or the amount of education received. The resultant sample represented (1) 32 states in the United States (Arizona, Arkansas, California, Colorado, Connecticut, Delaware, Florida, Georgia, Idaho, Illinois, Indiana, Massachusetts, Minnesota, Missouri, Montana, Nebraska, New Hampshire, New Jersey, New Mexico, New York, North Carolina, Ohio, Oklahoma, Pennsylvania, South Carolina, South Dakota, Tennessee, Texas, Utah, Virginia, Washington, and Wisconsin); (2) three Canadian provinces (Alberta, Manitoba, and Saskatchewan); and (3) five countries outside North America (Australia, Belize, England, the British Virgin Islands, and Venezuela).

After the sample was selected, we provided every supervisor with typed directions and a sheet of paper. At the top of each sheet was an example of sentences containing two indices of teaching expertise. (The example sentences were from Sacks and Mergendoller [1997] and described a general, or global, quality of a teacher and also an example of a specific behavior the teacher performed; see Appendix B for the form that was sent). The example statement was selected to illustrate that responses should focus on literacy teaching expertise rather than on materials or philosophical approaches. The intent was to ensure that supervisors' informed reflections were unrestrained, to implement the first procedure in a point-by-point Delphi analysis. Every step was taken to ensure that participants could express professional judgments in their most unrepressed and accurate manner. No attempts were made to influence any participant or suggest a priori categories upon which they were to reflect.

Each supervisor was allowed unlimited time (a second procedure in the Delphi methodology) to describe two traits (a third procedure for content validity and reliability of data collection) that *best* characterized the expertise that made a specific educator highly effective at a particular grade level. Every supervisor wrote two qualities that distinguished one highly effective literacy teacher, someone whom they had observed for longer than 3 years. Every supervisor was to judge "highly effective" based on indices of teaching experts derived from the body of research, as described in the theoretical background section of this Appendix (pages 125–128). In addition, a teacher had to demonstrate a high degree of success in advancing students' literacy abilities, as documented by their students achieving statistically significantly higher scores on state-level or standardized literacy achievement tests than students at their respective grade levels who took the same test at the same time in their own school buildings. Nominated teachers had to be teaching during the 1997–1999 school years.

Supervisors were to nominate teachers whom they had observed directly for 3 or more years and who had reputations with administrators, colleagues, and parents as being exceptionally effective in promoting literacy development. Every teacher was to exhibit the ability to stim-

ulate student enthusiasm for literacy, build literacy abilities for diverse students, and continuously strive to increase their own professional development. Each one would have also won
teaching awards for performance as a literacy educator and be held in high esteem by members of
the education profession.

After completing these descriptions, language arts supervisors stated (1) their own areas of
responsibilities, (2) the degrees held, (3) the grade levels that they had supervised, (4) the grade
level in which the highly effective professional that they described had taught, (5) the amount of
time spent in writing their descriptions of teaching excellence, and (6) their level of participation
at the 1998 and 1999 annual conventions of the International Reading Association. We collected
data statements for Phase I of this study from May 1998 to December 1999.

When the supervisors who met all of the above criteria were divided into groups that corresponded to the grades that their nominated teacher taught, the following breakdown occurred.
Forty-seven identified preschool teachers, 75 described kindergarten expertise, 112 recognized
first-grade indicators, 84 focused on second-grade, 152 noted third-grade qualities, 96 depicted
fourth-grade teachers, and 81 documented fifth-grade expertise.

Their list of qualities of literacy teachers' expertise was processed in an open coding (as opposed to a closed) format. The open coding enabled us to list every item as a new entry,
uncategorized. No priority ranking was given to any item, nor were any items grouped according
to any preconceived model. Items were typed verbatim into a database. No attempts were made
to interpret or alter the wording of any statement at this stage, or at any subsequent stage of the
research process, aside from the summaries created by the authors in Phase 3.

Phase 2: Collapsing Data into Categories

In Phase 2, the resultant 1,294 verbatim indicators of teaching expertise were listed by grade
level. Afterward, the authors and three research assistants "dimensionalized" the data. These assistants all held a master's degree in reading and had taught elementary literacy for 21, 14, and 11
years, respectively. We combined statements that described the same index of expertise into single items and tallied the number of people who recognized that quality at that grade level. For instance, several supervisors stated that preschool teachers possessed the ability to develop concepts of print by engaging students in listening to quality children's literature. When one teacher
wrote, "Develops concepts of print through asking students to listen to quality literature," and a
second supervisor stated that preschool teachers "taught concepts of print through reading children's literature to students," these two items were entered as a single entry of expertise in the
data pool and were tallied as two incidences of the same occurrence. We performed our categori-
zations independently. Combinations between raters were compared, and disagreements were
resolved through discussion. As a result, 44 categories of grade-specific literacy teachers' expertise were identified. Interrater reliabilities were computed by grade level. They ranged from 97%
to 84%, as reported in Appendix C.

Phase 3: Writing Summaries and Selecting Examples of Expertise at Each Grade Level

After a review of indicators at each grade level, we returned to the data and constructed integra-
tive memos of the most frequently cited indicators of practitioners' teaching expertise at each
grade level. These memos were designed to analyze whether categories of literacy teachers' expertise that were grade-level specific were related to particular domains of responsibility. The
raters identified six domains. For example, as shown in Appendix C, at every grade level there
exists a domain of responsibility within literacy expertise concerning how teachers plan, implement, and sustain lessons. These sets of actions were labeled Lesson Characteristics. All domains of responsibility arose from data; they were not presupposed by the authors prior to Phase
3 of the data collection process. We also combined the six domains into definitions of teaching expertise at each grade level and asked all respondents to reword items that did not clearly express

their intent. We selected two examples of activities from the statements in the database that characterized teaching expertise at each grade level. We resubmitted these activities to all respondents to ensure that they could be seen in the classroom of the expert that they had chosen.

Phase 4: Cross-Validation—Comparing Practitioners to Researchers

After a master list of teaching expertise, summaries, and examples had been reverified by practitioners through the Delphi analysis, data were submitted to an expert panel of researchers for their analysis and cross validation. We selected 17 university researchers who had not been involved in Phase 1, Phase 2, or Phase 3 of this study. Collectively, the panel had 134 years of experience in research, teaching, and directing professional development activities relating to literacy education. They had served as educators and literacy researchers in English-speaking universities and schools in Canada, Australia, Finland, Russia, Saudi Arabia, Germany, Mexico, and 16 states of the United States (Alabama, Arizona, Florida, Hawaii, Illinois, Indiana, Louisiana, Maryland, Michigan, Nebraska, Ohio, Oklahoma, Pennsylvania, South Carolina, Texas, and Wisconsin). They were selected using the following criteria. They had to be members of the Reading Hall of Fame, authors of articles in the Distinguished Educator Series for *The Reading Teacher,* authors of a chapter in the *Handbook of Reading Research,* or invited presenters at the International Symposium on Reading Instruction held at the University of Notre Dame in Indiana during the summer of 2000. Researchers were selected to represent the diverse range of knowledge bases that characterize elementary literacy research. Researchers were told that a list of characteristics of literacy teaching expertise by grade level was generated. They were not told how many people were surveyed, their geographical distribution, or their professional credentials to avoid biasing researchers' judgments. This also complied with a fifth criterion in cross validation through Delphi analysis—the anonymity of participants throughout the data collection and computation processes must be assured. We encouraged researchers to exercise the freedom to add items to the list if they so desired.

Researchers were given Appendix C, with the rankings of practitioners removed and items ordered randomly. Independently they performed the Delphi method of ranking items as to their level of importance at each grade level. Each researcher was to identify the five most important for each grade level. They were also asked to generate items that they deemed necessary if any item was not present on the initial list. Two of the 17 researchers generated 12 items not present on the initial list. As a result, 5 items were added to the grade 1 list, 2 to grade 2, and 3 items to grade 3. One item was added to the grade 4 list and 1 to grade 5. After these 12 items were added to the original list, data were resubmitted to the researchers. We asked them to reexamine the list and note if the addition of these items changed their initial rankings. No researchers altered their top five rankings. The goal of our cross-validation process was to compare practice to research and to determine whether the qualities identified by literacy supervisors were similar to those identified by university researchers.

Participants in all phases of this study gave thoughtful responses. Several indicators led us to this conclusion. Participants in Phase 1 averaged 21 minutes and participants in Phase 4 averaged 53 minutes to reflect and write. Participants in each phase also often explained the reasoning for their statements. For example, one researcher stated, "I can't rank grade 2 without adding two items concerning the importance of writing instruction. Expert teachers use writing to build second-grade students' quality of thought and their understanding of the purposes for writing conventions." Overall, it was felt that participants' answers tended to avoid clichés.

Results

Data provided answers to three questions.

1. *Do indices of teaching expertise differ by grade level?* Yes. Forty-four indicators of teaching expertise were specific to individual grade levels. These indicators are listed in Appendix C.

When data were compared across grade levels, indicators fell into six domains of responsibility. These domains varied in their rankings of importance but were present at every grade level. They were (1) the dominant role that experts assumed as classroom instructional leaders, (2) the strategies used to motivate students, (3) the talents called upon most frequently to reteach concepts, (4) the types of relationships built with students, (5) the qualities that teachers valued in the classroom, and (6) the characteristics of lessons taught. These grade-level qualities have been described in the text of this volume.

2. *Do researchers and practitioners agree on the qualities of teaching literacy expertise, preschool through grade 5?* For 87% of the qualities, the answer is Yes, as practitioners and researchers agreed on 70 of 88 initial categories as being the five most distinctive qualities of teaching expertise, per grade level, from preschool to grade 5. Thirty-two percent of the rankings by practitioners and researchers were identical. Moreover, researchers and practitioners agreed on at least one of the *two most important* qualities at every grade level. The rankings of both groups appear from first to fifth ("NR" indicates no ranking) in the right margin of Appendix C.

When the ordering of qualities of teaching expertise at each grade level was analyzed, additional data resulted. The order of domains varied by grade level. Data also indicated that talents at consecutive grades were not as closely related as were talents in *nonconsecutive* grades. For example, at the preschool, second-, and fifth-grade levels the first and second qualities of expertise were identical. At these grades, excellent literacy teachers were distinguished first by the qualities of the lessons taught and second by the characteristics of their classrooms. Differences emerged among these three grade levels at the third domain of teaching abilities. Preschool teachers differed from the latter two because their third most distinguishing quality was how well they motivated students. Second-grade teachers distinguished themselves from preschool and fifth-grade teachers because their third most important characteristic related to their abilities to effectively reteach concepts. Fifth- and third-grade teachers' expertise, at the third level, was distinguished by their ability to relate to students. The most distinctive pattern of expertise appeared at the third-grade level, which was the only one to have reteaching and motivation ranked as the two most important qualities.

3. *Can data about teaching expertise be obtained so that educators can make more informed decisions about directions to take to enhance their professional competencies?* Yes. Data demonstrate that highly effective literacy teachers, from preschool through grade 5, can be distinguished by how readily they executed specialized teaching behaviors and self-regulated their actions. These descriptions can be used by preschool to grade 5 educators to make more informed decisions about which grade level most consistently demands their talents so that they can most effectively meet students' literacy needs.

HOW THE SECOND STUDY WAS CONDUCTED: STUDENTS SPEAK UP ABOUT WHAT THEY WANT FROM THEIR TEACHERS

A second study was conducted during the 1999–2000 school year. This study involved 859 students from preschool through grade 5. Teachers know that they are an important force in their students' lives. They continuously work to nurture characteristics that correlate to high student achievement, and they value a student's opinion. The purpose of this research was to provide teachers with a student's perspective on what they deem to be the most important characteristics for a teacher to possess.

We wanted to identify what factors students think are most important in literacy instruction, even if these ideas related to minor adaptations on classes or lessons. Many teachers do not have time to stop to think about the small things that not only make a classroom more enjoyable for students but also increase productivity and achievement. We found that students think about them a lot.

The hypothesis was that teachers want to listen more to students' voices and opinions, but data about students' desires had not been collected. With these data, teachers would hear about improvements from "the mouth of babes." Regardless of how simple the desires were, we believe that data about students' concerns would be helpful to literacy success. For example, a second-grade student stated, "I wish my teacher would make different voices for characters in stories." Such a change might not even be considered unless students' voices were heard.

During the past 20 years, researchers have identified qualities that distinguish the most effective teachers, as discussed earlier. While this information is beneficial to becoming an effective teacher, implementing the opinions and suggestions that students have could also assist us to attaining the goal of true expertise. Our notion was that teachers who integrate their students' concerns and ideas in classroom instruction might realize a discernible increase in students' achievement, self-efficacy, participation, and motivation because they would realize that their teacher had listened to and implemented their ideas.

Method

Subjects were interviewed as to the qualities they most wanted in their literacy teachers. Students attended schools that served high, medium, and low socioeconomic neighborhoods, and they represented some 23 nationalities and ethnic origins. They lived in 28 states in the United States, thus representing a broad spectrum of the U.S. student population.

Specifically, the study included 73 preschoolers, 112 kindergartners, 135 first graders, 160 second graders, 126 third graders, 121 fourth graders, and 132 fifth graders. The method used was to provide students unlimited time to respond to the following prompt: "What do you want your teacher to do to help you learn more than you are now in reading?" "What can your teacher do to become a better literacy teacher?" Students in preschools, kindergartens, first, and in some of the second grade classes were asked to respond orally, while older subjects were asked for written responses.

Students were told that their teachers would not read their answers and that the researchers wanted to use their ideas to help other teachers improve their teaching of literacy. They were told to think about what the best teacher of literacy would do that would make it possible for them to learn more at their specific grade level. After these instructions were given, all subjects were allowed to write or speak as many ideas as they desired. In all cases the students' regular teacher was not in the room at any point during the study and data collection phases.

After all responses had been obtained, we compiled a listing by grade level of students' ideas. Then, independently we collapsed the data so that similar data were tallied together. To be collapsed, single statements had to refer to the same teacher action, only worded differently. Each tally was agreed upon by the same four raters who conducted the tally in the first study reported previously in this Appendix (page 130), and which resulted in a unanimous interrater reliability. Items that could not be read or understood were eliminated from the study, meaning that, of the original 1,314 statements, data in this study came from 1,189 of them.

Results

The most frequent response cited at every grade level was reported in this book in Chapters 5–10. These responses were direct quotes from students. Each statement was placed in the chapter that described the category of teacher actions to which a desire related.

Conclusions

In conclusion, our goal was to collect research about what students want their teachers to do during literacy instruction. Many studies have been conducted about what teachers believe their students need. The information in this book will move us forward toward making every classroom belong to both the teacher *and* the student. As previously stated, this work was done with a national sample of students. We recommend that teachers try to implement a comparable student survey in December and May of each year to receive student feedback on what they wish their teachers would do more of in class. If our work assists you in taking the first step toward making your classroom more encompassing and engaging from the perspective of students, our time involved in conducting these research studies will have been well spent.

Additional information about these studies can be found in Block (2003) and Block, Oakar, and Hurt (2002).

QUALITIES OF EXEMPLARY TEACHING BEHAVIORS DATA COLLECTION FORM[*]

Directions: The purpose of this study is to identify the qualities possessed and regularly exhibited by exemplary teachers of literacy. You have been selected because of your experience as a supervisor of literacy, active membership in the International Reading Association, and service in an English-speaking country. We ask you to participate in a Delphi analysis of exemplary teaching behaviors. To do so, you will need to complete the form below. The information on the first page of it will remain confidential. The answers that you provide will be analyzed anonymously. When all data have been tallied, we will ask you to confirm the accuracy of the data and to change findings that were interpreted inaccurately. If any member of the study alters data, these changes will also be submitted for your confirmation of accuracy.

PART I

Name _____

Title _____

School district _____

Address _____

City, state, Zip code _____

Phone number _____

E-mail _____

Fax _____

Three most recent attendances at the annual conventions of the International Reading Association _____

Number of years of supervisory experience _____

Number of years at current position _____

Grade levels that you supervise _____

Please read the following information and perform each requested action sequentially. Write the time that you have right now on your watch here _____.

PART II

Reflect until you have identified the best elementary teacher of literacy that you presently supervise and whom you have observed teaching literacy at the same grade level for at least three years. This teacher must have demonstrated exceptionality through his or her students' attainment of significantly higher test scores in literacy than students of other teachers in their same schools and socioeconomic environments. The teacher must have received teaching awards and high levels of respect from colleagues, administrators, and parents, and should demonstrate the desire to continuously improve his or her professional competencies.

Write the grade level that this individual teaches: _____.

PART III

Select the two most important behaviors that distinguish this exemplary teacher in his or her abilities to teach literacy at that grade level. State two characteristics that this teacher possesses that make this teacher effective at this particular grade level. These characteristics are the ones that you most credit for this teacher's success with increasing literacy achievement for the students in his or her classroom. From all of your experience, what teaching qualities are most distinctive at the grade level that you specified above? Your descriptions can be written in a global, all-inclusive format or can be written in a more specific manner. For example, Colin Sacks and John Mergendoller (1997) completed research concerning highly effective kindergarten teachers. They found that highly effective kindergarten teachers are exceptionally skilled at keeping students'

> "wonderment" alive by giving positive feedback to keep students' creativity and curiosity active (global quality). In one case a teacher rewarded students for "making signs for a castle made out of blocks during activity time" (specific behavior).

Take as long as you need to write your answers below.

Write the time that you have on your watch now that you have completed writing your answers _____.

A CONTINUUM OF INDICATORS
OF TEACHING EFFECTIVENESS

(Total participants = 647 language arts supervisors and 17 researchers)

PRESCHOOL

Preschool teachers (n = 47); interrater reliability = 97%

Lesson Characteristics

Teachers sing songs, chants, and poems with differences in tones, pitches, and body motions that are highly effective in helping emergent readers learn literacy concepts and the alphabet. Teachers help students memorize poems because students mimic their teachers' modeled speech. Teachers value that oral, responsive language must be modeled and practiced as a daily component in literacy development. Vocabulary is built through continuous repetition of spoken words in chants, songs, poems, and prose readings.

*Ranking**	
Sup.	Res.
1st (26)	2nd

Lesson Characteristics

Teachers develop concepts of print, letters, and sounds through students' listening to children's literature.

Ranking	
Sup.	Res.
2nd (19)	NR

Classroom Qualities

Teachers use movement and students' continuous, active, and sensory-based cognitive engagement to learn literacy concepts. They are masters at giving children the space to absorb and explore single letters, objects, sounds, smells, tastes, and words in their own time and for as long as individuals desire.

Ranking	
Sup.	Res.
3rd (13)	4th

Motivation

Teachers duplicate students' real-world activities at school more than educators at higher grade levels (e.g., they study ducks with live animals; take field trips to the pond; and participate in learning centers set up with prescription pads, feeding labels, incubators, and records of the number of days until the birth of ducklings mounted above the cage in large lettered words and numbers)

Ranking	
Sup.	Res.
4th (11)	NR

*Sup. (left ranking), ranking by literacy supervisors; Res. (right ranking), ranking by researchers; NR, no ranking. Numbers in parentheses are the number of literacy supervisors providing these descriptors.

Dominant Role and Talents   *Ranking*

Teachers welcome parents as active and meaningful participants in their   Sup.   Res.
children's literacy experiences. They model how parents can provide
continuous literacy learning throughout the evening hours. They make   5th (9)   3rd
family contacts and encourage complete family involvement in literacy
activities every day; they ensure that this happens daily more than
teachers at higher grade levels. They make home visits to leave family
literacy materials with caregivers.

Relating to Students   *Ranking*

Teachers are perceived by their students as friends, and school is viewed   Sup.   Res.
as a second home. Teachers establish a classroom climate that is just as
much an environment for students' self-esteem to be nourished as is a   NR (7)   5th
healthy home environment. Teachers care about the whole child's well-
being first and, when that is assured, take each one through the gate that
opens to the world of literacy. They use the children's fascination with
nature and their discoveries through sight and touch to provide a strong
base to praise and reward the value of successful discovery and to build
oral vocabulary. They know that the foundation for success is built by
guiding individual discoveries and not by tying all questions to (or with)
print.

Reteaching   *Ranking*

Use multiple experiences together in single lessons to help students   Sup.   Res.
experience learning together. Rarely is print, sound, smell, movement,
taste, or touch used singly as the only input system to reteach a literacy   NR (6)   1st
concept.

KINDERGARTEN

Kindergarten teachers (n = 75); interrater reliability = 97%

Classroom Qualities   *Ranking*

Teachers are intimately informed about developmentally appropriate   Sup.   Res.
practices and are always looking for research-based practices to enhance
print-rich curricula. Letters, words, and sentences are taught through   1st (41)   1st
print-rich environments that are often begun by the children. Teachers
write messages, notes, and signs. They help construct interactive letters
and charts as answers to students' questions. Teachers help children
explore, question, and learn concepts of print in animated ways, using
puppets and other physical objects.

Lesson Characteristics

Teachers honor and allow for the individual student's pace of learning. They use individual writing assignments and interactive writing experiences every day. Students and teachers write together (e.g., one-to-one instruction during journal writing activities and compose group thank-you letters). Students write what they can, and teachers write the rest. Teachers spell or write words that students request. Teachers or other adults are beside kindergartners as they scribble or write letters to say what they mean.

Ranking

Sup.	Res.
2nd (37)	3rd

Motivation

Teachers and their students enjoy humor and nonsense as long as everyone is being silly or moving at the same time (e.g., acting out silly songs and stories). Teachers have exceptional abilities to stimulate children to use imagination to act out stories and make predictions.

Ranking

Sup.	Res.
3rd (33)	5th

Reteaching

Teachers ensure that they, adult volunteers, or highly advanced peers are there until children gain confidence to write or pretend-read on their own. They use concrete objects and allow individuals more time to reignite interests in literacy. Student-centered teaching occurs daily, so many kindergartners are able to experience success. Phonemic awareness activities play an important role in the curriculum. Through the use of students' own language, voices, and books that students select and have heard repeatedly, teachers develop students' abilities to listen to, segment, and blend words. Literacy experiences are repeated frequently, using the same text and context.

Ranking

Sup.	Res.
4th (20)	4th

Relating to Students

Teachers incorporate real-life experiences to enhance children's experiential voids. Teacher(s) are adept at employing real-world experiences to develop oral and written language and to bolster students' own cultural backgrounds. Teachers praise the correct portions of answers.

Ranking

Sup.	Res.
NR (15)	2nd

Dominant Role and Talents

Teachers are highly skilled at using daily observations and not printed tests to guide their instruction. This instruction included at least one and not more than three concepts about print in any single setting. Teachers are exceptionally talented in teaching only what a class is ready to learn.

Ranking

Sup.	Res.
5th (14)	NR

FIRST GRADE

First-grade teachers (n = 112); interrater reliability = 95%

Lesson Characteristics

Teachers teach literacy all day. They are highly effective in integrating reading and writing instruction with every activity. Thematic units drive much of what is read and written by students. Writing occurs in the context of science and social studies instruction. Students have opportunities to use the skills they are learning throughout the school day. Teachers keep instruction relevant to students' lives, access their prior knowledge, use all available literacy resources, use literature in all subjects, and recognize the need to address multiple intelligences. By the end of the year there are high demands on most students with respect to the use of conventions. Students are taught to check their writing to determine whether their use of conventions is correct. Students are taught writing every day. This process approach most often results in reading more than one book and writing more than one final product a week. Students use resources that are constantly available around the room to plan, draft, and then revise as they read and write. One-to-one teacher conferences occur as a part of the revision and small-group reading processes. Editing sheets and cue cards for the writing process are always displayed. Teachers encourage the use of many decoding strategies.

Ranking

Sup. Res.
1st (63) 1st

Reteaching

Teachers communicate their high but realistic expectations. Teachers expect or demand that all students work up to their capacities every day. Students are expected to identify new words in books that they read. Teachers consistently establish two objectives to be practiced and assessed with each independent literacy practice session. For instance, when students begin to read orally, they say, "I am listening to how well you read in phrases like we just did together and how well you think about the meaning of words as you sound them out. I'll ask you to tell me the meanings of words that you are struggling to pronounce." Or, when beginning a sustained writing assignment, teachers will say, "I will check to see that you capitalize all sentences and end every sentence with a period, exclamation point, or question mark." Teachers gradually and steadily increase demands each day as the year progresses, using intense scaffolding with individuals as they use literacy skills and strategies. Students are continuously engaged in learning or practicing their literacy ability and not engaged in cutting and pasting or teacher-led drills most of the day. Scaffolding occurs effortlessly with an ease that these teachers are unable to even describe if questioned about their success.

Ranking

Sup. Res.
2nd (52) 2nd

Relating to Students

Teachers explicitly teach children to self-regulate. They give children input to decisions about their own learning by asking such questions as "Are you ready to proceed?" Teachers develop self-regulated, autonomous learners. They believe that first graders need to be aware of the printed word and that they can construct and decode it themselves. They praise and correct errors as learning-in-progress to avoid errors in learning as students attempt independent application of new concepts for the first time.

Ranking
Sup.   Res.
3rd (36)   NR

Classroom Qualities

Exemplary teachers nurture students and instruct with attention to creating the safest possible environment for attempting new literacy feats. They manage instructional pace and classroom routines through lessons that are exceptionally well matched to students' achievement levels. Teachers make frequent reference to classroom resources that can assist in spelling (e.g., easel displays and charts with words on them). When students publish their books, they do the input themselves on a computer. Students' writing is prominently displayed in the room. Instruction focuses on wordplay, using daily interactions with print involving tongue twisters, rhymes, and rereading of easy patterned text; students are encouraged to read along and then write. More frequently than in lower grades, the print-rich environment is designed for students to use resources independently.

Ranking
Sup.   Res.
4th (30)   NR

Lesson Characteristics

Teachers use synthetic phonics, onset-rhyme, and spelling strategies together, without denying children access to authentic and intrinsically valuable children's literature. Teachers demonstrate and require students to use their phonemic awareness skills in conjunction with context clues and each new decoding strategy introduced. They understand how to implement a broad-based literacy program that integrates many instructional approaches, such as using language and literature to teach phonics.

Ranking
Sup.   Res.
5th (20)   3rd

Dominant Role and Talents

Teachers are truly concerned about using many forms of assessment for students. They are masterful encouragers, supporters, and integrators. Teachers do not so much cue use of particular literacy independence skills at a particular moment to the entire class, but rather assist single students in choosing appropriate skills to be applied in the process of performing the literacy task at hand.

Ranking
Sup.   Res.
NR (12)   4th

Motivation

Teachers instill in each child the love of learning literacy as well as the will and enthusiasm to become lifelong users of literacy. They are positively enthusiastic about every child's accomplishment, no matter how seemingly trivial or small. They pack the day with a multitude of constant teaching in short segments. When motivation is low, they vary the breadth and depth of lessons and, when children are eager, teach up to 20 skills in an hour.

Ranking
Sup.   Res.
NR (11)   5th

SECOND GRADE

Second-grade teachers (n = 84); interrater reliability = 96%

Lesson Characteristics

Teachers are exceptionally talented at creating new ways to teach basic decoding, comprehension, and fluency strategies. They continuously reinforce phonetic principles in oral and written language situations that arise naturally. They create wordplays, word sorts, and many new types of current events games so that students can continue to enjoy learning how to read and write. They use journals and writing lessons to teach reading and vice versa.

Ranking

Sup.	Res.
1st (52)	1st

Classroom Qualities

Teachers create an exceptionally relaxed, positive learning environment that challenges students to think on a deeper level. Teachers begin to visually display how classroom literacy instruction honors diversity and teaches students to accept the consequences of making mistakes during reading and writing. Teachers have an exceptional ability to bridge the gap between students who are still emergent readers and those who are more established, while keeping them all interested and engaged. They integrate reading and writing through learning centers and throughout the entire classroom.

Ranking

Sup.	Res.
2nd (41)	2nd

Reteaching

By second grade, there are a variety of reading levels represented. In order to reach all children, teachers are exceptionally skilled in flexibly helping students develop a sense of responsibility and independence, yet are available to them when they need guidance and assistance individually. They use one-to-one conferences and tutor often. They use manipulatives, music, graphic organizers, and read-alouds from excellent children's books and poetry to help accomplish this goal. They reteach to let children know they can succeed with a strategy tried unsuccessfully in earlier years. Teachers are masters at adapting to diverse learning styles. They are very creative and quick on their feet, constantly thinking of new ways to demonstrate and explain the same concept over again in a new light.

Ranking

Sup.	Res.
3rd (27)	3rd

Motivation

Exemplary teachers inspire a love of learning and reading by re-creating less able readers' joy through creativity. They galvanize new sparks of interest and excitement to make reading an important part of students' lives. They set a goal to make every child's day more exciting than the day before. They help children make connections to what they already know as the first step in their literacy lessons. They demonstrate how much adults enjoy and value literacy so students can come to value it as well.

Ranking

Sup.	Res.
4th (15)	NR

Relating to Students   *Ranking*

Teachers encourage substantive conversations and encourage children to   Sup.   Res.
share their insights and learn from one another. They realize that   5th (13)   NR
children learn through talk and that they create meaning through
discussion. They make transitions to content areas with personalized
guidance. Teachers' instruction is used frequently to (1) portray the
power and pleasure that is gained by reading books, (2) complete a direct
modeling, and (3) initiate a guided practice session or individual work.

Classroom Qualities   *Ranking*

Teachers distinguish themselves by continuing to maintain a print-rich   Sup.   Res.
environment.   NR (8)   4th

Dominant Role and Talents   *Ranking*

Teachers most often use demonstrations by an adult or expert   Sup.   Res.
(themselves or able students), because they have found them more   NR (12)   5th
powerful than direct instruction in separate skills for students at this
stage of literacy development. The goal of every lesson is for teachers to
stimulate and allow students to extend themselves to learn more literacy.

THIRD GRADE

Third-grade teachers (n = 152); interrater reliability = 93%

Reteaching   *Ranking*

Teachers engage in a variety of activities to reteach, enrich, and review   Sup.   Res.
concepts. They develop higher-level word-attack skills, feed into   1st (63)   1st
students' interests to make reading fun and exciting daily, and teach to
broad areas of interest to keep students responding to literature. They
remember that third-grade children continue to learn through concrete
hands-on experiences as frequently as younger students, and they turn to
them to reteach. They use numerous types of poetry and fun stories to
capture interest and teach figurative language. They have an excellent
knowledge of standards and incorporate them with reviews through
game-like activities. They meet the educational needs of a class
characterized by widely diverse ability levels. Teachers assess the ability
level of each child. They cultivate a new content interest and use it to
carry students over obstacles that block their individual learning curves.
They have the ability to repeat, repeat, and repeat without getting blue in
the face, and at the same time they use phrasing and instructions that
students consider to be "cool." They are also very knowledgeable about
language skills, so they are able to expertly answer the discussion
questions that emerge when students are reading and writing.

Motivation   *Ranking*

Teachers actively work to motivate and engage students to keep the   Sup.   Res.
excitement of reading alive. They encourage them by helping them   2nd (55) 2nd
realize that they can turn to print to locate answers even when they lack
the self-confidence to do so; they improvise, using dramatic
representations of a character in the story. They keep students
interested in reading by introducing new authors, leaving students
curious, encouraging their interest in character development, and able to
read with increasing fluency and ease. Teachers consider being able to
keep things interesting and engaging as one of their most important
objectives. Teachers must possess the ability to express their excitement
over reading and writing by bringing to life materials read in the
classroom. Students realize that their teachers are teaching them
strategies that are important, so they exert extra effort because they are
committed to and trust their teachers. Teachers are also willing to
explore unusual turns of events that capture the attention of students.

Classroom Qualities   *Ranking*

Teachers have the ability to handle a group of children who are at a wide Sup.   Res.
range of levels, so that most students learn to read longer books—   3rd (47) NR
perhaps their very first chapter books—under the teachers' skillful
management and instruction. They are masters in managing a class so
that students do lots of reading to themselves and one another. The
teachers explore their interests independently and in groups. They also
design the class so that students have time to think.

Relating to students   *Ranking*

The teachers are exceptionally gifted in expressing their genuine care Sup.   Res.
and interest in students' social and emotional development. They notice 4th (45) 3rd
moods and attitudes. They let students know they understand what they
are asking beyond the words that they say. They trust their students to
ask questions without fear. They have insight into each learner's needs,
built through acceptance, caring, and empathy with individual learners.

Lesson Characteristics   *Ranking*

Teachers have the ability to stimulate deeper thinking about text by   Sup.   Res.
asking students to defend their positions. They develop critical thinking NR (38)   4th
skills and lead students toward learning how to read a textbook
independently with high levels of comprehension. They encourage them
to take risks. Teachers use their own passion for learning as a model to
develop independent, critical thinkers. They possess exceptional talents
at moving students from dependent to independent learning. They can
simultaneously make abstract concepts concrete while creating an
undying sense of purpose in students' quest for comprehending subjects
at very deep levels. They also have to depend on their abilities to explain
more clearly the expectations for each activity in order to elicit quality
participation. For those with difficulty in decoding, they use different
words and phonics instruction until students discover that reading
consists in uniting together a lot of different components.

Dominant Role and Talents	*Ranking*	
	Sup.	Res.
Teachers demonstrate exceptional expertise in making transitions from learning to read to reading to learn. They build a bridge between learning to read and reading to learn and capitalize on the understanding that it may be the last year that many students have to learn to read. They realize that many teachers beyond third grade view literacy instruction as a tool with which to learn. They teach how to gather information from text and help students transfer reading skills to content areas. They teach students how to transition from picture to chapter books and do their best to accommodate individual learning styles and needs. They allow third-grade students to close the gap between early (basic) literacy skills—to evolve into more skilled readers—by helping them move from a "little kid to big kid" mentality. Teachers build upon students' backgrounds by using multileveled materials. They locate material that enables students to read words but with enough substance to draw students' minds into authors' purposes, points of view, and content. They have a passion and love for bringing the written word to life. Teachers are exceptionally gifted in assisting students in feeling that all things are possible. Teachers add their own personal touch to teaching, one in which they manage and guide proactively as a whole person. Teachers are gifted managers. They are structured and possess the ability to plan and present a variety of learning activities at the same time. They are well organized and adept at juggling a packed curriculum; they use time efficiently to work with a variety of ability levels and incorporate multilevel reading, knowing that not all students learn the same way. These teachers are among the most able users of flexible guided-reading groups.	5th (38)	5th

FOURTH GRADE

Fourth-grade teachers (n = 96); 87% interrater reliability = 87%

Dominant Role and Talents	*Ranking*	
	Sup.	Res.
Teachers demonstrate distinguished themselves in their ability to effectively teach students how to pull information from a textbook, apply strategies beyond literature to content areas, and use comprehension strategies in science and social studies with high levels of critical thinking. Their most distinguishing quality is their ability to simultaneously instruct numerous students during the same lesson (i.e., to aid those who are still learning to read, to push those reading to learn, to teach new tools to those who want to pull more information from text and use higher-level thinking skills with content area texts, and to establish longer-term projects for those ready to become experts in a subject topic). They do so by differentiating between goals as assignments are introduced, choices of books are made, and time is allocated to instruction. They coach students to facilitate responsible learning and to make students realize that they are responsible for the extent to which they learn.	1st (52)	1st

Lesson Qualities

Ranking

They continue to teach students to be independent learners while working on long-term projects. They introduce numerous goals, teach a variety of strategies in the same lesson, and allow students to select one that best matches their learning style in order to become independent readers and responsible for their own learning. They are highly skilled at focusing lessons on larger goals such as becoming better citizens and helping in the world.

Sup.	Res.
2nd (38)	2nd

Relating to Students

Ranking

The teachers have an exceptional ability to restate students' negative comments in positive ways. They rechannel negative attitudes toward literacy or their literacy abilities in a positive manner. They distinguish themselves in their ability to identify students' talents rapidly and to focus lessons on these talents. They model and invite students to share their ideas and to develop thoughts by asking questions and supporting their ideas. They ask questions instead of telling. They readily make connections to an individual student's personal experiences. They are exceptionally kind, approachable, and willing to invest extra time after school hours to learn how best to relate to students at their own level.

Sup.	Res.
3rd (29)	NR

Motivation

Ranking

To achieve a high level of student involvement in literacy, the teachers share many exciting educational activities that open new vistas on students' worlds and interest areas outside class. They are gifted in finding "teachable moments" and going with them, and they base each new concept on something that pertains to one or more students in the class. They are experts at keeping students engaged with topics, interested, and wanting to learn by moving goals up or down the cognitive scale instantly.

Sup.	Res.
4th (27)	5th

Classroom Qualities

Ranking

The teachers' basic principles of teaching are to expose students to real-world events to guide students' literacy development. Their goal is to have students make lifelong commitments to reading and to making the world a better place to live. They help them relate reading skills to the role that these serve in constructing and living a fulfilling and successful life. Themes abound about vital human conditions. They coach students in locating resources that enable them to make consequential decisions with the information that they read.

Sup.	Res.
5th (23)	3rd

Reteaching

Ranking

The teachers are highly skilled at teaching critical thinking. They teach students to apply inferential thinking to reading. They teach students how to incorporate reading strategies into everything that they read and how to think for themselves, ask questions, and seek answers. They model thinking on a deeper-than-surface level. Independent reading and comprehension instruction are stressed. Learning to think on a high plane, under their leadership, becomes "cool" and fun.

Sup.	Res.
5th (23)	4th

FIFTH GRADE

Fifth-grade teachers (n = 81); interrater reliability = 89%

Lesson Characteristics	*Ranking*	
	Sup.	Res.

Teachers instill in students a desire to autograph their work with excellence. They teach them how to organize their thoughts and to explore and learn on their own. They teach students how to ask for guidance and set boundaries within which students can best achieve higher levels of literacy through self-governance. They are nonjudgmental. Their goal is to guide and shape students' thinking and comprehension strategies in reading and through reading. Teachers empower students to take chances; they hold debates in class, allow students freedom and choice, and meet students' individual needs more easily. They have the ability to mix structure with freedom. They empower students to do something important. They make students prove their points. They have a strong commitment to advancing both their students' knowledge and character.

Ranking — Sup. 1st (49) — Res. 3rd

Classroom Qualities	*Ranking*	
	Sup.	Res.

The teachers are organized and spend time before each day begins ensuring that everything in place so that the day runs smoothly. They are highly skilled in planning. They do not waste time. Every year they have more to teach and less time to do it. They meet students' needs while teaching content topics that must be covered—along with the many extras at this grade level—and having less time to teach them. Teachers are flexible, having to overcome the elective classes and speakers that take chunks of time out of the daily schedule. They cover vast amounts of material while simultaneously stimulating students' deep interest in, and high levels of understanding of, concepts that are taught.

Ranking — Sup. 2nd (33) — Res. 2nd

Relating to Students	*Ranking*	
	Sup.	Res.

The teachers are in touch with the many impulsive needs of fifth graders, and they are adept at working with students who sometimes feel as though they know "everything" about how to read. They use a sense of humor to relate to students. The teachers are able to laugh, and they have the ability to think like a fifth grader. Teachers understand a broad range of learning and maturity levels. They have the patience to help those students who work "outside the box," that is, outside the usual guidelines.

Ranking — Sup. 3rd (32) — Res. 4th

Dominant Roles, Talents, and Motivation   *Ranking*

The teachers are expert in many content areas. They have the ability to   Sup.   Res.
cover vast amounts of material in a limited time so that students end up   4th (30) 1st
understanding what was covered. Teachers are exceptionally talented in
using new research to bring enthusiasm to the classroom and enable
students to get into the subject matter, whether the content pertains to
the Revolutionary War, astronomy, or decimals. They enjoy and are adept
at dealing with a wide range of topics and adapting them to learnable
chunks. They use a variety of higher-level thinking questions to stay one
step ahead of their students. They have expertise in developing a parallel
focus that is of equal importance—using literacy to develop students'
critical thinking abilities and to increase resiliency in students' self-
esteem and self-efficacy as readers and people. They relate real stories to
the curriculum and stimulate students to relate their lives to the
curriculum. They are masterful storytellers and dramatists. Their classes
are fun, active, and exciting. They teach two subjects during the same
period; otherwise, they would not have enough time to reach every
content area and literacy goal. They do so by instructing in a manner that
makes students want to use what they read to produce something new.
They demonstrate sensitivity and may vary the time that they spend
teaching a concept anywhere from 15 seconds to several days, as
students' needs warrant.

Reteaching   *Ranking*

The teachers convey abstractions through analyzing a content domain to   Sup.   Res.
emphasize its critical components. They do not depend only on concrete   5th (18) 5th
examples. They instill their love for literacy and distinguished literature
by teaching students how to analyze a story's structure, predict outcomes
for a novel, and use the writing process to express the depths of their
thinking about literacy and various topics. They are highly skilled at
engaging students in stimulating responses to books by delving into many
layers of meaning that students have never examined before.

REFERENCES

Allington, R. L., Block, C. C., & Morrow, L. (2000, April). *Effects of departmentalization and non-departmentalization on fourth-grade reading achievement*. Paper presented at the annual meeting of the American Education Research Association, San Francisco, CA.

Allington, R. L., Guice, S., Michelson, N., Baker, K., & Li, S. (1996). Literature-based curriculum in high-poverty schools. In M. Graves, P. Van den Broek, & B. Taylor (Eds.), *The first r: Every child's right to read* (pp. 73–96). New York: Teachers College Press.

Anders, P. L., Hoffman, J. V., & Duffy, G. G. (2000). Teaching teachers to teach reading: Paradigm shifts, persistent problems, and challenges. In M. L. Kamil, P. B. Mosenthal, P. D. Pearson, & R. Barr (Eds.), *Handbook of reading research* (Vol. III, pp. 719–742). Mahwah, NJ: Erlbaum.

Archer, J., & Blair, J. (2001). Performance testing being readied for Ohio teachers. *Education Week, 20*(19), 14.

Atkin, J. M., & Black, P. (1997). Policy perils of international comparisons: The TIMSS case. *Phi Delta Kappan, 79*(1), 22–29.

Au, K., & Carroll, J. (1997). Improving literacy achievement through a constructivist approach: The KEEP demonstration classroom project. *Elementary School Journal, 97*, 203–221.

Ayers, W. (1996). *Teacher's lore*. New York: Brown.

Baumann, J. F., Hoffman, J. V., Moon, J., & Duffy-Hester, A. (1998). Where are teachers' voices in the phonics/whole language debate: Results from a survey of U. S. elementary teachers. *The Reading Teacher, 50*, 636–651.

Benner, P. (1986). *From novice to expert*. Reading, MA: Addison-Wesley.

Bents, M., & Bents, R. (1990, April). *Perceptions of good teaching among novice, advanced beginner and expert teachers*. Paper presented at the annual meeting of the American Educational Research Association, Boston.

Berliner, D. C. (1994). Expertise: The wonder of exemplary performance. In J. N. Mangieri & C. C. Block (Eds.), *Teaching thinking for teachers and students: Diverse perspectives* (pp. 163–186). Fort Worth, TX: Harcourt Brace.

Berliner, D. C. (2001). Mentoring, teaching, and competency. *Educational Leadership, 58*(8), 10–15.

Berliner, D. C., Stein, P., Sabers, D., Clarridge, P. B., Cushing, K., & Pinnegar, S. (1988). Implications of research on pedagogical expertise and experience for mathematics teaching. In D. A. Grouws & T. J. Cooney (Eds.), *Perspectives on research on effective mathematics teaching* (pp. 70–77). Reston, VA: National Council of Teachers of Mathematics.

Biddle, B. J. (1997). Foolishness, dangerous nonsense, and real correlates of state differences in achievement. *Phi Delta Kappan, 79*(1), 9–13.

Block, C. C. (2001a). The case for exemplary instruction: especially for students who begin school without the precursors for literacy success. *National Reading Conference Yearbook, 49,* 421–440.

Block, C. C. (2001b, May). *What can we do to increase teacher change?* Paper presented at the annual convention of the International Reading Association, New Orleans, LA.

Block, C. C. (2001c, December). *It's not scripted instruction but personalized instruction that makes a difference in students' literacy success.* Paper presented at the National Reading Conference, Scottsdale, AZ.

Block, C. C. (2001d). Thinking development during reading instruction. In A. Costa (Ed.), *Developing minds* (3rd ed., pp. 292–298). Alexandria, VA: Association for Supervision and Curriculum Development.

Block, C. C. (2003). *Teaching comprehension: The comprehension process approach.* Boston: Allyn & Bacon.

Block, C. C., Joyner, J., Joy, J., & Gaines, P. (2002). Process-based comprehension: Four educators' perspectives. In C. C. Block & M. Pressley (Eds.), *Research-based best practices* (pp. 119–134). New York: Guilford Press.

Block, C. C., & Mangieri, J. N. (1996). *Reason to read: Thinking strategies for life through literature.* Boston: Pearson.

Block, C. C., Oakar, M., & Hurt, N. (2002). The expertise of literacy teachers: A continuum from preschool to grade 5. *Reading Research Quarterly, 37*(2), 178–206.

Bond, G. L., & Dykstra, R. (1997). The cooperative research program in first-grade reading instruction. *Reading Research Quarterly, 32,* 345–408. (Original work published 1967)

Borko, H., & Livingston, C. (1988, April). *Expert and novice teachers' mathematics instruction: Planning, teaching and post-lesson reflections.* Paper presented at the annual meeting of the American Educational Research Association, New Orleans, LA.

Brown, J. S., Collins, A., & Duguid, P. (1989). Situated cognition and the culture of learning. *Educational Researcher, 18,* 32–42.

Bruner, J. (1986). *Actual minds, possible worlds.* Cambridge, MA: Harvard University Press.

Bullough, R. (1989). Case study of a teacher's transition from novice to advanced beginner. *Dissertation Abstracts International, 22,* 11–12.

California Congressional Record. (1988, March 30). *Rationale for California educators: Peer review assessment program,* line 73.

Cazden, C. (1994). *Whole language plus.* Portsmouth, NH: Heinemann.

Chi, M. T. H., Glaser, R., & Farr, M. J. (Eds.). (1988). *The nature of expertise.* Hillsdale, NJ: Erlbaum.

Costa, A. (Ed.). (2001). *Developing minds* (3rd ed.). Alexandria, VA: Association for Supervision and Curriculum Development.

Degroot, A. D. (1966). *Thought and choice in chess.* The Hague, The Netherlands: Mouton.

Dillman, D. (1978, April). *Teaching effectiveness.* Paper presented at the annual meeting of the American Educational Research Association, San Francisco, CA.

Duffy, G. G., & Hoffman, J. V. (1999). In pursuit of an illusion: The flawed search for a perfect method. *The Reading Teacher, 53,* 10–16.

Elias, M. J., & Tobias, S. E. (1990). *Problem solving/decision making for social and academic success.* Washington, DC: National Education Association.

Erickson, K. A., & Smith, J. (Eds.). (1991). *Toward a general theory of expertise.* Cambridge, England: Cambridge University Press.

Expert Panel Testimonies Transcript. (1998, June 23). *Regional state board of education open forum report:* Sacramento, California State Department of Education, p. 39.

Faust, M. A., & Kieffer, R. D. (1998). Challenging expectations: Why we ought to stand by the IRA/NCTE Standards for the English Language Arts. *Journal of Adolescent and Adult Literacy, 41,* 540–547.

Flippo, R. F. (2001). *Reading researchers in search of common ground.* Newark, DE: International Reading Association.

Glaser, R. (1987). Thoughts on expertise. In C. Schooler & W. Schale (Eds.), *Cognitive functioning and social structure over the life course* (pp. 113–132). Norwood, NJ: Ablex.

Glaser, R. (1990). Expertise. In M. W. Eysenk, A. N. Ellis, E. Hunt, & P. Johnson-Laird (Eds.), *The Blackwell dictionary of cognitive psychology* (p. 97). New York: Macmillan.

Good, T., & Grouws, D. (1975). *Process-produce relationships in 4th grade mathematics classes.* Columbia, MO: University of Missouri College Education.

Harter, H. (1899). *Developing expertise.* New York: World Book.

Hawkins, A., & Sharpe, T. (1995). Field system analysis: In search of the expert pedagogue. *The Journal of Teaching in Physical Education, 31,* 221–234.

Hoffman, J. V., Mccarthy, S. J., Elliott, B., Bayles, D., Price, D., Ferree, A., & Abbott, J. (1998). The literature-based basals in first-grade classrooms: Savior, Satan, or same-old, same-old? *Reading Research Quarterly, 33,* 168–197.

Housner, L. D., & Griffey, D. C. (1985). Teacher cognition: Differences in planning and interactive decision making between experienced and inexperienced teachers. *Research Quarterly for Exercise and Sport, 56,* 44–53.

Humphrey, T. (2003). *In the first few years: Reflections of a beginning teacher.* Newark, DE: International Reading Association.

International Reading Association. (2000). *Excellent reading teachers: A position statement of the International Reading Association.* Newark, DE: Author.

Juel, C., & Minden-Cupp, C. (2000). Learning to read words: Linguistic units and instructional strategies. *Reading Research Quarterly, 35,* 458–493.

Knapp, M. S. (1995). *Teaching for meaning in high-poverty classrooms.* New York: Teachers College Press.

Krabbe, M. A., & Tullgren, R. (1989, March). *A comparison of experienced and novice teachers' routines and procedures during sedentary and discussion instructional activity segments.* Paper presented at the annual meeting of the American Educational Research Association, San Francisco, CA.

Lee, C. (2001, April). *Teacher interventions for students with learning disabilities.* Paper presented at the annual meeting of the American Educational Research Association, New Orleans, LA.

Leibert, R. E. (1991). The Dolch List revisited. *Reading Horizons, 31*(3), 217–227.

Leinhardt, G., & Greeno, J. (1986). The cognitive skill of teaching. *Journal of Educational Psychology, 78,* 75–95.

Mangieri, J., & Block, C. C. (Eds.). (1994). *Creating powerful thinking in teachers and students: Diverse perspectives.* Fort Worth, TX: Harcourt Brace.

McCombs, B. (1995, April). *Exploring components of motivation.* Paper presented at the annual meeting of the American Education Research Association, San Francisco, CA.

Medley, D. M. (1977). *Teacher competence and teacher effectiveness: A review of process–product research*. Washington, DC: American Association of Colleges for Teacher Education.

Michel, P. A. (1994). *The child's view of reading*. Boston, MA:

Moll, L. (Ed.). (1990). *Vygotsky and education: Instructional implications and applications of socio-historical society*. Cambridge, England: Cambridge University Press.

National Board of Professional Teaching Standards. (1997). *Standards for National Board Certification. Report 113*. Princeton, NJ: Educational Testing Service.

National Captioning Institute. (1990). Thinking aloud. In *The new English teacher: A guide to using captioned television with language minority students* (p. 6). Vienna, VA: Author.

National Commission on Teaching and America's Future. (1998). *What matters most: Teaching for America's future*. New York: Teachers College Press.

National Reading Panel. (1999). *National Reading Research Panel Progress Report to the National Institute for Children's Health and Development*. Washington, DC: National Institute for Children's Health and Development.

Nelson, K. R. (1988). *Thinking processes, management routines and student perceptions of expert and novice physical education teachers*. Unpublished dissertation, Louisiana State University, Baton Rouge, LA.

Ohio State Department of Education. (1999). *Complete teacher academy: Preparing tomorrow's teachers today*. Columbus, OH: Author.

Palaco, P. (2002). *The butterfly*. New York: Scholastic.

Polya, G. (1954). *How to solve it*. Princeton, NJ: Princeton University Press.

Pope, W. (1866). The confederation question from the Prince Edward Island point of view. *The Islander*. Retrieved from *www.hpedsb.on.cal/coll/Fathers/pope.htm*

Porter, A., & Brophy, J. (1988). Synthesis of research on good teaching. *Educational Leadership, 45*(8), 74–85.

Pressley, M., Allington, R., Wharton-Mcdonald, R., Block, C., & Morrow, L. M. (2001). *Learning to read: Lessons from exemplary first-grade classrooms*. New York: Guilford Press.

Pressley, M., Rankin, J., & Yokoi, L. (1996). A survey of instructional practices of primary teachers nominated as effective in promoting literacy. *Elementary School Journal, 96*(4), 363–384.

Rankin-Erickson, J. L., & Pressley, M. (2000). A survey of the instructional practices of special education teachers nominated as effective teachers of literacy. *Literacy Disabilities Research and Practice, 15*, 205–225.

Rosenshine, B., & Furst, N. (1971). Research on teacher performance criteria. In J. Brophy (Ed.), *Research in teacher education* (pp. 414–442). Englewood Cliffs, NJ: Prentice-Hall.

Roskos, K., Risko, V. J., & Vukelich, C. (1998). Head, heart, and the practice of literacy pedagogy, *Reading Research Quarterly, 33*, 228–239.

Ruddell, R. B. (1997). Researching the influential literacy teacher: Characteristics, beliefs, strategies, and new research directions. In C. K. Kinzer, K. A. Hinchman, & D. J. Leu, Jr. (Eds.), *Inquiries in literacy theory and practice: 46th yearbook of the National Reading Conference* (pp. 37–53). Chicago: National Reading Conference.

Sacks, C. H., & Mergendoller, J. R. (1997). The relationship between teachers' theoretical orientation toward reading and student outcomes in kindergarten children with different initial reading abilities. *American Educational Research Journal, 34*(4), 721–739.

Sartain, H., & Stanton, P. (1974). *Report of the Commission on High-Quality Teacher Education*. Newark, DE: International Reading Association.

Schon, D. (1983). *The reflective practitioner*. New York: Basic Books.

Shuell, T. (1990). Phases of meaningful learning. *Review of Research in Education, 60*, 531–548.

Smith, N. B. (1989). *History of reading instruction*. New York: World Book.

Snow, C. E., Burns, M. S., & Griffin, P. (Eds.). (1998). *Preventing reading difficulties in young children*. Washington, DC: National Academy Press.

Vygotsky, L. (1962). *Thought and language*. Cambridge, MA: MIT Press.

Vygotsky, L. (1967). Play and its role in the mental development of the child. *Soviet Psychology, 12,* 62–76.

Warwick, D. P., & Lininger, C. A. (1975). *The sample survey: Theory and practice*. New York: McGraw-Hill.

Wertsch, J. (1991). *Voices of the mind*. New Cambridge, MA: Harvard University Press.

Wilkinson, I. A. G. (1998). Dealing with diversity: Achievement gaps in reading literacy among New Zealand students. *Reading Research Quarterly, 33,* 140–161.

Wilson, S., & Ball, D. L. (1997). Helping teachers meet the standards: New challenges for teacher educators. *Elementary School Journal, 97*(2), 121–138.

Wolcott, H. F. (1988). Ethnographic research in education. In R. M. Jaeger (Ed.), *Complementary methods for research in education* (pp. 187–249). Washington, DC: American Educational Research Association.

Worthy, J. (1996). A matter of interest: Literature that hooks reluctant readers and keeps them reading. *The Reading Teacher, 50,* 204–212.

Worthy, J. (2000). Conducting research on topics of student interest. *The Reading Teacher, 54,* 298–299.

INDEX